I0816434

WHAT MATTERS IN LIFE

Lessons I Learned from Opening My Heart

ICHAK K. ADIZES

books@adizes.com
Website: www.adizesbooks.com

For information, please contact WS Press by email at wspi.353@gmail.com

First Edition
ISBN: 979-8-9860483-3-8
Library of Congress Control Number: 2022944109
Published by WS Press, Newtown, PA
Printed in the United States

This book is dedicated to my teacher, the late Master Chariji; to my wife, Nurit Manne Adizes, without whose teaching and love I would not have been able to create; and to my son, Nimmy, whose love inspires me.

Acknowledgements

I want to thank Yechezkel Madanes, who organized many of my writings into a book; Teena Apeles, who edited it; Jessica Hoffmann, for copyediting; Larry Schiller, who led me and trusted me to write this book, and his assistant, Collin McCarthy. Thank you all.

Contents

PART III: Self-Development

Introduction

In March of 1943, three generations of my family were living in Skopje, Macedonia—the birthplace of Mother Teresa—when they were sent to a death camp in Treblinka, Poland. My parents and I survived the Holocaust, escaping to Albania, while all those we loved were burned alive. I closed my heart for most of my life. I feared love like a burn victim fears fire. It was too dangerous to love. Those I loved perished.

All my energy went into building a successful career. Over five decades, I developed an effective methodology for managing change without destructive conflict (The Adizes® Symbergetic™ Methodology for Managing Change). Unlike a consultant who makes recommendations that an organization is expected to follow, my methodology is to ask the right questions, in the right sequence, until the organization comes to its own realization—its own answers.

Since the 1970s, my work has taken me to all corners of the globe, serving organizations and governments in more than fifty countries. I was successful but not happy. I could not feel love. I decided I would not give up and live my life without experiencing love. I worked on opening my heart, about which I reported in my memoir

The Accordion Player: My Journey from Fear to Love.[1] What is success without love?

As I've traveled the world, I've collected insights, many of which I've been publishing in blog form on my website, ichakadizes.com. The blog posts focus on love, relationships, marriage, parenting . . . what really matters in life, the insights I got as I was opening my heart.

This book is an edited compilation of those blogs. It is not the reporting of results from scientific research. It is a collection of insights from what I've read, seen, heard, or felt in unpredictable yet fascinating ways as I've met with people around the world, on issues affecting us as human beings. I pride myself on learning from everyone.

The purpose of this book is not to preach or teach. Rather, I share my thoughts with the hope that they will invite and stir reflection and debate, but more importantly, to help you realize what matters in life—and how to not only protect it, but make it flourish.

This topic is of particular significance nowadays, with atrocious wars in different parts of the globe. We are living in a uniquely challenging era of accelerated change and continuous technological disruption. We have never been as interconnected. Yet we are experiencing more loneliness, depression, and relationship failures than ever before.

What do we do to overcome these challenges? How do we handle this new normal of continuous change and the disintegration it is causing? What is the role of love in this new world? And what is love to begin with? What are its essential ingredients? How is love expressed? How do I begin to love again?

Ichak K. Adizes, Ph.D.
Santa Barbara, California
2022

[1] Adizes, I., *The Accordion Player: My Journey from Fear to Love*, 2023.

PART I

Love

Love Yourself First

Can you hear your heartbeat? It is beating for you.

I was six years old when my family was taken to a death camp during the Holocaust. After the war, we immigrated to Israel in 1948. We arrived penniless. I had to work from the age of eleven to support my family after my father, a longshoreman, broke his legs, and was not earning enough. My family could only afford to eat one meal a day of bread and cheese.

All in all, I had no carefree childhood. I did not know what it was like to just have fun and do nothing. I never did. I did not know what it was to just be happy. I never experienced that.

NURTURE "LITTLE YOU"

I once met with a neurolinguistic coach whom I told my story. She asked if I had a picture of myself from the time of the war. I found one. I was six and standing on a street in Kosovo, holding the strings of a rope I had dismantled to look like shoelaces, trying to sell them to earn money so I could bring home food. I look sad and scared. "Take care of Izzy [my nickname in Yugoslavia, my birth country]," the coach told me. She suggested I take that picture with me wherever I go and commit myself to nurturing this little kid who never had a childhood.

"To take care of Izzy, imagine you are his father now," she told me. "What would you do for him?"

I was in Bled, Slovenia, and that afternoon I took Izzy for a walk around the lake, surrounded by very tall mountains populated by trees. I imagined holding his hand, and we talked for a long time. I bought him an ice cream. I told him not to be scared anymore, that I would be there for him as long as I live. And that I would never let him down. I told him that I loved him very much and hoped that he would eventually smile, because life does offer opportunities to smile and love.

I had the best time ever.

I hugged little Izzy and promised to take him on another walk soon.

What happened here?

"Izzy (Me)" and "I" are not the same. "I" need to take care of "Izzy (Me)."

"I" taking care of "Me" is not only for those who had no childhood. It applies to every human being. "If you do not take care of yourself, who will? And if not now, when?" asks Rabbi Akiva, a Jewish sage who lived during the latter part of the first century.

ARE YOU IN TOUCH WITH YOUR HEART?

I remember a doctor once gave me his stethoscope to listen to my own heart. He asked me: "Can you hear your heartbeat? It is beating for you. Are you in touch with your heart?"

Realizing I had been taking my heart for granted, I became teary-eyed. I realized I also took my kidneys for granted, as well as my lungs. They were all working very hard to keep me alive, and yet I had never stopped to ask them, "Hey, how do you feel?" They were there with me from the day I was born—like little Izzy has been with me—but I had never paid real attention to them. They were "there" somewhere, like passengers on a car I drove. They were not "Me." They were "Them."

I discovered that the thing I identified as "Me," throughout my life, was only my brain. As if I was just a walking brain. All the other parts of myself were secondary. They were not properly integrated in my Being and were therefore neglected.

And what is absolute integration?

LOVE. Love has neither space nor time boundaries.

I needed to love myself, every part of me without exclusion of any part of me, as a condition to free energy to love the world. Instead of looking "out there" to find love, I realized I needed to do the work "in here," starting with "little me."

Before going on to love others, you need to be able to love the little Izzy in you.

When you get up, ask your heart, "Hello, how are you today?" And your lungs, and your body. And your emotions too: "How do we feel today?"

Start the day "together." Otherwise, in the rush of modern life, we disintegrate: the body goes one way, the mind another way, and the emotions suffer.

MAKE IT YOUR FULL-TIME FOCUS

I noticed that people who have difficulty showing love to others also have difficulty accepting love from others. They squirm when someone shows affection. They are uncomfortable with intimacy. When a person tries to get close to them, they find ways to undermine, or even flee the situation. It is too threatening. It's as if they feel obligated to reciprocate if someone loves them, and the whole experience of a loving, reciprocal relationship seems outside their comfort zone.

Once we love ourselves, it frees the energy to go into the world and love others. Yet to love others, you must first allow others to love you.

The result is a most painful dilemma. On the one hand, there is a great desire for love. After all, love is a basic human need that we all have. But at the same time, it's frightening. We end up desperately wanting, and then desperately pushing away, what we so deeply desire.

One unfortunate result of this conflict is that we edge away and choose the wrong person as a life partner, a person who cannot show love either. Or we marry someone who loves, but we push them away and reject their love repeatedly. In both cases, it is to the detriment of having an intimate, caring relationship.

What is the cause of this behavior? In my case it was caused by the fact that loving and being loved was an exceedingly painful experience, causing wounds and scars, depriving me of joy and happiness.

The people I love (or who love me) can disappear; love can end up being very scary. As the title of a best-selling book by Gerald G. Jampolsky, MD, puts it, *Love Is Letting Go of Fear.*

Can you?

What do you fear?

What Is Love?

Love is a muscle. You have to exercise it.
You have to make it grow or it atrophies.
—Chariji, Master, the Sahaj Marg Mission

Romantic books and movies depict love as an emotion—a feeling that you cannot overcome. Religion looks at love as something spiritual: God loves you.

But there is more to robust, sustainable love than just emotions.

LOVE HAS MANY FACES

It is not enough to feel love.

The loving is expressed through action; it's not enough to just *feel* love. What do you do to express your love? In the Jewish religion, it's essential to make *tzedaka*, which means to do something righteous, be charitable, and help people in need. And you should make your donations anonymously. You should do it with all your heart and not expect anything in return—not even recognition. When you work your land, you should leave a tenth of the field unharvested. Leave it for people who need to feed themselves.

Love is, thus, not only a feeling; it should also be expressed in the *doing*. In love, the reward of giving is in the giving itself. The more I give, the more I get.

One has also to behave in a way that adheres to the symbols of behavior that manifest love, like bringing flowers or gifts, recognizing anniversaries, and being trustworthy in your actions and respectful in your communication.

And love should not be static. That's why Chariji, the Master at the Sahaj Marg Mission in the Himalayas, says, "Love is a muscle. You have to exercise it. You have to make it grow or it atrophies. It's not static."

So, love is an emotion, granted—but do not take love for granted. In order to maintain that emotion, it is not enough to only feel. For sustainable love, you need to express it in action, be respectful and trustworthy, and feed it so it grows.

How about love as a system of values?

Love is the harmony of different voices singing in unison, complementing each other, with mutual trust and respect. It's a workable unity. There is no love without mutual trust and respect.

My whole philosophy of organizational change and relationship is based on building and nurturing mutual trust and respect. There is trust when we share common values and interest. As to respect, Immanuel Kant, the philosopher, says it is to recognize the sovereignty, that is, the undeniable right of the other person, to think, to be, different. You're Italian. I'm French. It's fine. You don't have to be like me. You're a Muslim, I'm a Christian or Hindu. We don't have to be the same. We respect each other's differences.

We show disrespect when we prohibit people from thinking or being different.

Why is mutual trust and respect desirable? Because we learn from differences. We do not learn from people who think exactly like us. If two people agree on everything, there is nothing to learn. You learn from people who disagree with you, the ones who are different from you. But that will happen if we respect their right to think differently. And trust should be there. Because without mutual trust, respecting other people's difference in opinion might not be easy.

YOUR HEART KNOWS

Life presents problems. They have a function to perform.

Problems test mutual trust and respect. Can we decide together, respectfully? And do we trust we have common interest to implement the decision?

Finding mutual trust and respect will not happen in the thought process. When we listen to our minds, we encounter debates: pros and cons on any issue. When our hearts speak, there are no questions, no doubts, and no disagreements. No cost-benefit analysis. We are complete, we are One, we are at peace. That is why the expression "with all my heart" resonates.

Try, to start with, letting the heart—not the brain—tell you whether you can respect and trust the other person.

Why not the brain? Some people think that their thoughts are their own and that they truly can lead them to make the right choices.

I suggest that our thoughts are not just ours. We absorb what the media tells us is right and what our peers tell us is wrong and vice versa. We pick up thoughts on the street, opinions derived from experiences both good and bad, starting from childhood, from our dreams about the future. So not all our thoughts are just ours. What is genuinely ours is not easy to carve out by thinking. That is why many people wonder, even throughout their lifetimes, who am I, really? What do I really want?

I suggest that what we feel in our hearts is uniquely ours. That is who we really are.

When we meditate and listen to the heart, we often find answers to problems we couldn't solve by thinking. In meditation it just comes to us as a realization. Interestingly, it happens also in our sleep. We go to sleep with a problem and wake up in the morning with an answer we could not have reached by thinking about it the previous day or days.

Why in meditation? Why in our sleep?

To listen and hear the whispering of our hearts, we need to block the distracting noise of our thoughts.

When we are calm and willing to listen, what is that voice that's whispering from the heart? It's telling us which decision feels right and which feels wrong. It knows whom to respect and who is trustworthy. Your heart knows. You know.

Threats To Love

Love is continuously tested.

Life is full of surprises. And a significant amount of the surprises can be very upsetting. As time passes, our needs and expectations change. People's moods and feelings change. With change we have problems we need to solve together, and we find ourselves in some passing conflict with the one we love, and what happens? The one we love is not as loving and giving or attentive. It often feels like rejection. The rejection hurts, and many make a mistake in how they react to this temporary withdrawal of love. We reciprocate by also withdrawing our love and now we are both in pain. We both withdraw, and this mutual withdrawal, if repeated, can become permanent. The deeper our love, the more painful the confrontations are, the more probable the withdrawal.

The withdrawal is painful because love is rewarding and pleasurable. Thousands of poems have been written about love and how wonderful it is. The more rewarding it is, the more painful the withdrawal will be. It is the pain of its loss that makes people fear love, just the way that someone who was badly burned will not get close to a fire.

CAN THERE BE LOVE WITHOUT TEARS?[1]

Some people avoid the pain by avoiding falling in love. They avoid the pain but in the process avoid the heavenly pleasure of being in love.

To love, one must live with periodic pain. It comes with the territory, which we call life. There will be ups and downs in the relationship.

People or things you love will not always give you pleasure. On the contrary, they can give you pain, too, and the more pleasure they give you, the more pain you feel when that pleasure is missing. And it will be missing from time to time because life is change. As time passes or conditions change, the things or people you love might not always be there as you want them to be, when you want them to be.

There is no love without some pain. You will be unhappy from time to time. Love anyway, despite the reality that your love might periodically cause you pain. Do not withdraw your love today. Wait and see what happens tomorrow. And next week.

Anyone who expects ongoing love—or the presence of a soul mate who only loves and where the feeling is only up, up, and up—is living in a dreamland. If you are deeply in love and hope, pray, believe that this feeling is going to last forever, you will be disappointed. That feeling will not last forever.

What is up will come down. And the higher it rises, the lower it will descend.

Reality is change. And change is life. And life is filled with challenges that test love. Can you handle change? Can you tolerate a temporary rejection?

Do not fall into the trap and assume that love is forever and then, when life and change test the relationship, become surprised that

[1] Inspired by the phrase "*zar bez suza ima ljubavi,*" a Serbian song.

there are challenges to love. What should be committed to forever? What is the essential precondition for love? A commitment to mutual trust and respect.

Ask yourself and you partner: Are we committed to never break each other's trust? To respect each other no matter how much we disagree? To avoid using harsh words, put-downs, and offensive tones?

Do not ask yourself how committed you are to love. Ask yourself how committed you are to mutual trust and respect.

If you are, love will come back even though there is a threat to it in the short run.

Someone once told me that if you are ever upset with your beloved, just wait a day or two before confronting them. Just let time pass. The situation may change, the mood may change and, all at once, what gave you so much pain two days ago now feels ridiculously insignificant.

The story is different if the loss of trust and respect is ongoing and becoming a pattern that is not changing. In that case, no matter what we say to each other, there is no more love.

The essential ingredient of love is mutual trust and respect. Without it love evaporates. Thus, pay attention to the foundations of love. In all confrontations the guiding light is mutual trust and respect. No matter how difficult the problem is you are trying to solve, never solve it with a process that threatens trust and respect. Better to have a so-so solution without losing mutual trust and respect than to have a first-class solution reached with mutual disrespect and tarnished trust.

And this does not apply only to love between people. It applies to loving oneself. As we have problems we need to solve by ourselves, we have conflicts in our own heads, too. We might feel unloving to ourselves by losing our self-trust and self-respect.

RESPONDING WITH ANGER

All interpersonal problems are caused by either the unsuccessful search for love or the denial of love.

All we do in life, beyond what we need to do to survive—like working to secure food and shelter—is for love. What is our need for appreciation and respect, if not a camouflaged need for love? And what is the average complaint, if not a desperate call for love?

When we perceive that we are being denied love, we get angry—a powerful emotion that tends to fire up rather quickly and can become very destructive. It is as if love is expected to be there no matter what, like air to breathe. We might not express our anger vocally there and then, but it shows in our body posture, in the tense voice with which we express ourselves.

According to Reiki, a form of energy healing developed in Japan by Dr. Mikao Usui during the 1920s, anger is caused by fear. And when we fear, we attack proactively to defend ourselves.

Each time you are angry, ask yourself, what is it that you fear?

If you remove fear, you remove anger.

If anger is a manifestation of a fear—in this case, the fear of not being loved— wouldn't it be more appropriate if, when a loved one expresses anger, you could "see through" the anger and show your love rather than reprimanding and correcting the other person?

How would you treat an angry baby? Would you punish them for acting out? Or would you hug and comfort the baby in order to calm them down? Why not treat our partners and loved ones of any age the same way?

Imagine your partner yelling at you. The usual response would be to yell back. What would happen if you said nothing and just went over and hugged them, just as you would hug a baby? Try responding with love, not anger.

All interpersonal problems—and maybe personal problems, too—are caused by either the unsuccessful search for love or the denial of love.

In the United States, hospitals sometimes bring to a patient's bedside a dog, trained to lick the patient's hands and sit still to be petted. Showing and receiving love heals.

As the expression maintains, "Love conquers all. Love heals."

If you accept the differences of your beloved and show your trust of them, love will flourish. Thus it is imperative to nourish and defend mutual trust and respect. Whenever I experience an ongoing challenge to trust and/or to respect—when hurt feelings don't pass after waiting a day or two—I try to address it promptly and without delay. If not, it percolates below the skin, so to say. It is an emotional infection that may erupt one day without warning, and often without a clear reason. Never go to sleep angry with your loved one. Take steps to address these feelings instead of letting them potentially percolate in isolation. Spend the night, if necessary, clearing up issues of trust and respect until they are clarified.

Find ways to communicate your feelings to your loved one. Respectfully. Avoid raising your voice. Before you speak to them, it helps to breathe. Take a piece of paper, and write down all your hard feelings. Writing has the potential to free the energy that is stuck in you, as you are angry.

Try calming the mind down before you open your mouth. When your stomach is churning and you're upset, speaking can be difficult. The stomach and the mouth should not be acting at the same time. Calm down first.

If you are unable to do so as a couple alone, mediation or therapy is called for. Denial—hiding the problem—does not work

The key to solving problems lies in how *you solve them, not whether you actually have the right solution.*

In solving problems, make sure not to ruin mutual trust and respect. Years later, you won't remember what the solution was, but you will never forget how it was solved, how the interaction made you feel. Be open and do not withhold information and how you feel even though it might stir a painful discussion. There is nothing more powerful to feed mutual trust and respect than being genuinely open.

What destroys a relationship is not what we argue about but what we do not talk about.

DENYING FORGIVENESS DENIES LOVE

Love and forgive.

Once a year on Yom Kippur, Jewish people fast and pray, atone and forgive ourselves for sins and misdeeds, and ask forgiveness of others. By the time the day is over, we are supposed to start the new year guilt-free. And during that daylong fast, our love of God is repeatedly confirmed.

Judaism also emphasizes the power of forgiveness when we bury our loved ones, precisely at the moment when people may be angry at God for having taken their loved one forever. In that case, the prayer—the Kaddish, *Yitgadal veyitkadash shmay rabba* ("Glorifed and sanctified be God's great name")—reconfirms the love of God nevertheless. Love and forgive.

Without forgiveness, love suffers to the point that love might disappear and be replaced with hate—of others, or of oneself.

Those who cannot forgive, those who hold on to guilt or blame themselves or others, end up spending a great deal of unnecessary and negative energy that "eats them up" and makes them sick. The worst energy sucker is hate. It ages us prematurely.

The solution is to love deeply and honestly so that you can forgive yourself and others.

Do not try to understand. Just forgive.

Love without questioning. Without cost-benefit calculations. Just forgive. Unconditionally.

Let's explore the different possibilities of how to love and forgive.

- *Forgive first. Love second.* ("I will love you if I can forgive you.") This is conditional love. It does not work, but many of us do it because to hate and keep a grudge is easier than to forgive and love.
- *Love first. Now forgive those you love.* It works, if it is a true, honest, non-judgmental, non-needy love. Like a loving parent forgives a little child. The parent forgives because they love their child unconditionally.

But here is the catch: The more you love a person, the more difficult it may feel to forgive them.

It is easier to forgive someone you do not know very well, while it is very difficult to forgive those whom you are close to. The closer emotionally a person is, the more difficult it is to forgive them. That is why family feuds are so painful and prolonged. That is why divorces are an emotional disaster.

Why is it not easy to forgive those we love or those we expect to love us?

Because of expectations. We expect those we love or are loved by to behave a certain way, and when they do not, we go to war. We cannot forgive them easily. We have no expectations from people we do not know well. Forgiving or ignoring them is relatively easier.

TAKING THOSE YOU LOVE FOR GRANTED

Neemanot makot ohev (Hebrew).

The pain inflicted on us by the one who loves us is the most painful one.

The people we admonish the most and scold the most—and thus give the most pain to—are the ones we love the most.

It should be just the opposite, right? The ones you hurt the least should be the people you love. So why do we hurt them the most?

We all have strengths and weaknesses. And whom do we love? Those who complement us and exhibit strengths in areas where we are weak. Yet we get upset when they don't share our dominant skills. We forget that they are not us. And they criticize us for what we are weak at and they are strong at. And the relationship swerves to a dead end—sometimes to a complete breakdown.

My suggestion: Change your mindset.

Stop expecting from others the excellence you expect from yourself.

You chose your partner or friend because their strengths are your weaknesses. By the same token, their weaknesses are your strengths. So by definition, they are not you. By definition, they cannot do as well as you can do in certain realms.

Use your strengths to help your loved one with their perceived weaknesses, and your partner should use their strengths to help you with your weaknesses.

What if you stopped criticizing their weaknesses and started dealing with them with your strengths?

BECOMING A PRISONER TO YOUR EXPECTATIONS

Love without conditions.

Sahaj Marg, meaning "the Natural Way" or "Heartfulness," is a meditation practice that focuses on the heart. I practice it. It has a prayer.

To paraphrase the prayer, it says: "Oh Master, you are the true goal of human life. It is expectation that blocks our way to you, and you are the only power that can make us reach the goal."

The prayer confused me. I do not like a personality cult that preaches to be like the Master. And how can the Master be the power to reach the Master?

After much discussion with the spiritual leader Daaji, I came up with the following interpretation:

Who is the Master?

God.

What is God?

God is love, absolute love.

Let's then replace the word "Master" with the word "love."

The prayer will then read: "Love, you are the true goal of human life. It is expectation that blocks our way to you, and you, love, are the only power that can make us reach the goal."

Why is love the goal of human life?

Because what is love? Absolute integration. We are one. An enduring union. No time or space breaks our integration. When we love someone, even after they have passed away, we feel as if they are next to us. We still talk to them and exchange views. The time dimension does not exist, and since we listen to their advice even though they are not next to us physically, the space dimension does not exist, either. No matter how far away the person we love is, we still feel them as if they are near.

Love is total integration beyond time and space.

In total integration, there are no barriers, no conflict that wastes energy. The result of such total integration is happiness and, according to many philosophies and religions, happiness has always been the goal of humanity.

But why would expectations and wishes block our way to love and happiness?

Because wishes and wants mean that we are short of something. We are missing something—thus, we wish for something else or want something else.

Expectations are more than just wishing and wanting. They insinuate a certain level of certainty. Of controllability. It is beyond wanting. The expectation assumes that the expected should be given.

An expectation is one of the steps on a ladder to hate.

First, you wish. It is just wishful thinking. When you escalate to wanting, it is now beyond just wishing. You are now using a stronger word by saying, I *want* this. When you move to expecting, you express a dimension of controllability: you believe you control the conditions that can fulfill your wishes or wants and, thus, you expect fulfillment.

You can escalate further from expecting to demanding, and then to deserving. And if you do not get what you believe you deserve, hate might ensue.

You wish, then you want, then you expect, then you demand, and the last step in the escalation is entitlement. And if you do not get what you feel you are entitled to, the next step is anger, and anger is disintegration. That's why wishes, if they progress, are antithetical to love; they disintegrate us. You feel you are not where you want to be. You are not integrated in the moment, and without integration, there is neither love nor happiness.

To expect is to give power to whatever or whomever you expect anything from. It disempowers you. You become a prisoner of your expectations. And no prisoner is happy in their prison.

Love is an overwhelming, powerful experience, especially when it comes with expectations. We say to our beloved: "I *need* you. I *cannot live without* you and you are *the only one*." We expect them to give love. To be there. To never leave. And this dependency, these expectations, imprison us, making us unhappy and continuously worried.

The way to be free is to say, "I do not need you that much and you are not the only one."

What happens now? You have removed the danger of having pain, of being punished, in a sense, when your beloved does not respond as you expected. But you have also removed the reward of being in love.

How do you avoid the pain of love and still have the joy?

Erich Fromm, the famous psychologist, prescribes the following: Do not say, "I love you because I need you." Say, "I need you because I love you."

Do not love because you need someone. That is where love becomes a power game.

Love independently of need. Love without depending.

Love should be independent of needs. Love because you *are* a loving person. Nothing to do with needs. Love without question, without limits, without conditions, without expectations. Love as a natural, ongoing response to being.

Love is not based on expected rewards, emotional or otherwise. It is what it is. It is like breathing. You do not compute the value of breathing. You just breathe. No one can take it away from you as long as you are alive. The same applies to love.

Be loving as a person. It is who you are. It is not a response to anything. It is what it is, and it is never too late to love.

The end of my rendition of the Sahaj Marg prayer is even more interesting: ". . . love is the only power that will bring us to love."

How come?

The road to love is with love.

You cannot get to greater love without some starting point of love, and the more love you give, the more love you have.

FALSE SENSE OF SEPARATENESS

Be different, together.

Have you noticed people who love their work, but their family is falling apart? Or people who love their country, but hate humans (racists, for example)? Or people who are very loving to others, but hate themselves?

Religions, political parties, and businesses all have a sort of brand symbol. Christians have the Cross. Jews, the Star of David. Muslims, the Crescent Moon and Star. What could be the brand symbol for a loving humanity as a whole, regardless of religion, race, culture, nationality, political affiliation, or sexual orientation?

The brain has in general two parts to it. The left is where we think and act. The right is where we create and feel. The right brain is related to the left hand, and the left brain to the right hand. When clasping our hands together and bowing to each other we are seeking to integrate our minds because we have our own conflicts of perceptions and wishes that can paralyze us.

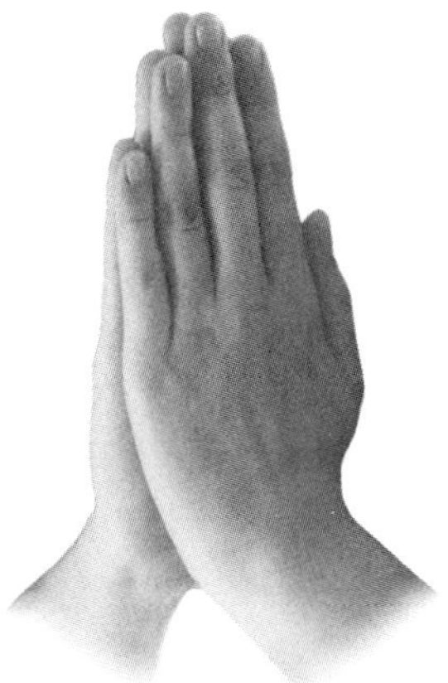

The Gyan mudra, a hand gesture used in Hinduism and Buddhism, involves taking the thumb and putting it together with the pointer finger. What does it symbolize? My interpretation is the pointer finger symbolizes masculine energy, ordering us where to go, what to do, and the like. The thumb is the only finger that can touch the tips of any of the other fingers. It's the finger that turns all the others together into a hand. Without a thumb, there is no hand. To me, a thumb symbolizes feminine energy, which is what makes a house a home, the energy that integrates the family. The Gyan mudra that brings the pointer finger together with the thumb, I suggest, can be seen as a symbol of the integration of the male and female energies as a loving couple.

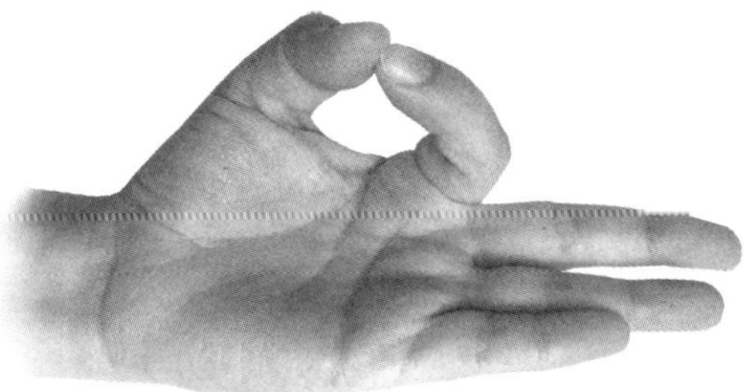

Now what about an extended hand, with fingers close together? That's often found in religious imagery. What do you see? Fingers of different sizes, yet all together, united. In Southwest Asia and North Africa, that symbol is called the *hamsa*. It is a blessing. What is its meaning? Be different but together. That applies to society, to the community, to the world at large.

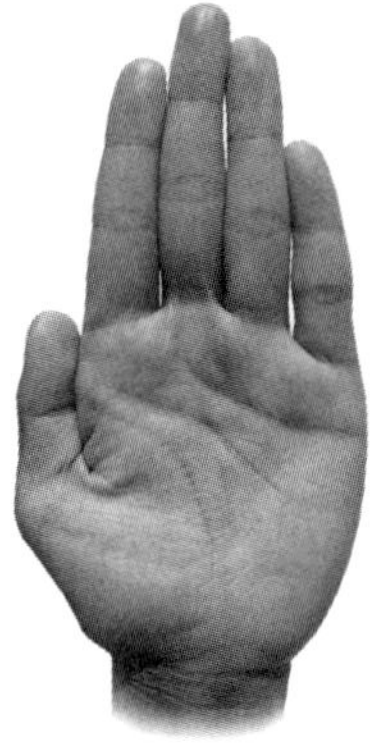

Now imagine if people would greet each other in the following way: hands together in a prayer, followed by the Gyan mudra, and then by an extended hand with fingers close together (the *hamsa*). That series of actions would communicate: integrate yourself first, integrate your relationships with your loved ones next, and then integrate humanity. That is the correct sequence to love.

How To Love

To feel happy or unhappy is a choice we make.

What is the difference between pleasure, happiness, and love?

Everyone wants to be happy. The U.S. Declaration of Independence states that everyone has an inalienable right to pursue happiness. But how do people pursue happiness? How do you find love?

CHOOSE LOVE FIRST

Myth: You will be happy if you are healthy.

There's the physical aspect of this belief: you will find happiness in a healthy body. This has caused the exercise industry to mushroom. People are jogging and stretching and puffing, but how happy are they? Being physically healthy is a desired condition in order to be happy. It may be considered necessary, but it is not a sufficient condition.

And there's the mental side to the myth: to be happy overall, you need to be *emotionally* healthy. Some people are addicted to seeking happiness through personal-growth workshops. It might provide some temporary relief but not a sustainable happiness.

Another myth: Happiness is a life without conflicts.

This is an utopian expectation. We fall in love with people who complement us, thus, by definition, they have a different style, different personality. Conflict comes with the love. It is a package. Can you find happiness by avoiding the inevitable pain of having to relate to someone else, perhaps a spouse, whose style is different from yours?

The difference between love and pleasure is the difference between liking and loving:

You like because of. *You love in* spite of.

You can avoid conflicts by living in solitude. Even that is a maybe because you will have conflict in your own head. There will be conflict between what you want to do, what you believe you should do and what needs to be done regardless.

Human beings are not solitary animals. We are social animals. We congregate. In prison, isolation is a punishment. Running away from relationships is running away from one problem to fall into another: the problem of solitude, loneliness, and a sense of failure.

Many equate pursuing happiness with pursuing pleasure. We may pursue pleasure by maximizing sex, seeking the richest food, driving expensive cars, smoking, drinking, and taking consciousness-altering drugs. But does pleasure bring happiness? Does it bring love?

Instead of expecting pleasure to bring happiness and happiness to bring love, I believe the sequence should be in reverse: love first. It will bring you happiness. And happiness will bring the pleasure of being happy.

HAPPINESS IS A CHOICE WE MAKE

In a YouTube skit, an American comedian claims he can achieve successful therapy in five minutes or less. In the script, a woman arrives in his office and tells him that she's always been terrified of being buried alive.

He says, "Just stop it. That will be fifty dollars, please."

She is shocked: "What? Fifty dollars for 'Just stop it'?"

"Yes," he says. "Just stop it."

There is a truth to the comedian's joke. Another story might make that clear.

There was a father who had two sons. One was an absolute optimist, and the other one was an absolute pessimist. The father decided to do some experiential therapy to help them change their extreme frames of mind. He put the pessimist child in a room filled with toys that most children only dream about, to help him realize that life is not so terrible: it can be wonderful to play and have a good time.

He put the optimist child in a room full of horse manure, to let him know that life is not always perfect: there's plenty of horse manure.

A few hours later, he visited each child's room to see what was going on. The pessimist child was bawling his heart out. "How terrible life is," he complained to his father. "So many toys! How can I choose which toy to play with? Why did you put me in this terrible situation only to suffer?"

On the other hand, he found the optimist child whistling, singing, laughing, and happily shoveling horse manure from one part of the room to another.

The father asked him, "Why are you so happy?"

"Because with so much horse manure, there must be a pony around," the optimist replied.

We choose how to feel.

To feel happy or unhappy is a choice we make. I've noticed that some people are always more or less happy. To them, everything is fine. They find the pony in every problem. Conversely, other people see only problems. (Confession: I am one of them. It makes me a great consultant but not a happy traveler in life.)

We decide whether to be unhappy or happy. Thus the first joke has some kernel of truth in it (otherwise it would not have been funny). "Just stop it" meant change your outlook. That is all. Obviously, if you can; if not, someone has to help you change your mindset. Instead of always seeing the glass as half empty, notice that it is also half full.

The question is, who is this "we" that has to change the mindset? Who decides, who makes the choice, when and how is the choice made? What is the mechanism that controls the choice?

LET THE HEART WIN

I have been observing people for many years, and I have realized that if the brain makes the choice, there is a high probability that the person will end up unhappy.

Why is that? Because the brain resides either in the future or in the past. Both can make us unhappy. The past cannot be relived, and its mistakes—or tragedies—cannot be prevented or corrected retroactively. And there is so much uncertainty about the future; it can generate fear and thus unhappiness.

The more cerebral the person is, the unhappier they may become. Less cerebral people, living in the here and now, seem happier. They let the brain rest and focus on the heart. They think less and feel more.

Thinking makes the individual analyze and rationalize, and either one can trigger a negative mindset. Feeling is different. You feel the trees as you pass them; you feel the clouds floating over your head. You don't wonder how the clouds are made or why they are shaped in a particular way. No thinking: you just feel the clouds, feel the mountains, feel the trees, feel the flowers, feel the people—without judgment.

I believe it is in feeling that we find happiness, but only when we don't fight what we feel. We just accept it and enjoy the wonders the world offers. The entry point to feel love? Just feel. Do not fight what you feel. Leave the brain alone. When you feel, you get integrated with what you feel. And in that integration, you find a sense of happiness and, through it, love.

The philosopher René Descartes is famous for the Latin dictum *cogito, ergo sum* ("I think, therefore I am"). My suggestion is to replace it with *ego sentio, ergo sum* ("I feel, therefore I am").

One of many reasons we fight fiercely over ideas and points of view is because we use only the brain and don't listen to the heart.

We reason with the mind. We feel with the heart. The mind produces thoughts and communicates with words. The heart communicates with feelings.

We differentiate right from wrong in our heads. We form and base our opinions on a myriad of conflicting messages from different sources: friends, family, teachers, books, and experiences. We often tend to suppress what our hearts are telling us and what feels natural. We suppress what our conscience says and use *only* our brains to justify our deeds.

The key to break this tendency is to detach yourself from your mind and to intentionally *feel*. To stop the brain for a moment and ask: Does this the opinion I am defending, the decision we are about to make, etc.—does it feel right, or wrong?

Right and wrong should not only be judged *but be felt as well.*

Not everything needs to be explained. Not everything needs to be understood. Not everything can be understood. The heart is connected to some absolute wisdom and conscience—the source of love—that if allowed to be felt, can be accessed, and can guide us in decision making. Feelings generated by the heart vet the distortions that the mind typically creates when it's used exclusively. The heart—where we feel—is innocent, pure, and clean, and can act through feelings as a conduit to absolute knowledge and conscience.

Respect means trying to be willing to learn from others. So, in watching them speaking, ask yourself what there is to learn from their thoughts. Then ask yourself how you feel about what you learned. Often you learned something new. It made sense. But in your gut, it did not feel right. And you do not even know why you feel the way you feel.

Follow your feeling. It comes from the heart and the heart knows best.

The heart must watch what we think, not only in meditation but all the time. The mind shouldn't be allowed to govern your life alone.

Anger, commonly believed to be just a feeling, always has thoughts fueling it underneath. There are always *reasons* people cite as the source of their anger. When a person truly stops thinking and reasoning, and just loves unconditionally, what happens to anger? It dissolves.

Anger and love cannot share the same space.

And if the mind and heart are in a conflict you can't resolve, let the heart win.

STOP THE DAILY GRIND

We often hear people complain that they cannot find the love of their life.

Many live in large cities, amid intense hustle and stress. They may have dogs or cats—something to greet them with unconditional love, without expectations, when they get home.

The pace of modern life drains the necessary energy required for love with another person. In order to have that energy, there must be peace and quiet. You must feel complete to be available to receive another person.

Have you ever heard of someone falling in love while running late, trying to catch a plane, or dealing with a crisis at work? Do you find love in noisy, deafening music?

We fall in love on vacation, or sitting next to someone on a plane with nothing to do but feel each other's presence and have a peaceful talk. We fall in love when we are at peace, when we are walking on the beach at sunset, when our energy is united into one big core. When there is noise, we get distracted, which disintegrates us. Disintegration is the antithesis to love, to total integration.

In order to find love, it's necessary to stop the daily grind.

And by the same principle, in order to keep the love you have, it's required to periodically stop running, and to experience some peace together.

I once heard an expression that goes, "the devil is in the hustle." The counter expression should be, "love is in peace and quiet and in feeling safe."

COMMIT TO LOVING ACTIONS

Love them the way they want to be loved.

There are books on "the languages of love" that claim different people expect love to be expressed differently. Some prefer being touched.

Others expect more time to be spent together, and others prefer presents as an expression of love.

I observed another differentiation: masculine personalities and feminine personalities interpret love differently. Not only do their interpretations of love differ, so do their expectations about how love should be expressed within their relationship. That often becomes one of the sources of conflict.

We are different. And we have to learn how to treat and love each other differently.

A feminine person bringing flowers to a masculine partner does not generate the same response (nor the same feeling of love and gratitude) as a man bringing flowers to a woman.

Women who show love by hugging and kissing, but criticize their masculine partner, tend to miss the target. He will feel disrespected, and thus not loved, even though he is hugged.

Those with masculine energy desire love to be expressed in respect and trust from their partners. That is paramount. Those with feminine energy want respect and trust, too. But their focus or emphasis is for their partner to take some time to demonstrate that they care.

Love should not necessarily be expressed in the way you want to be loved, but in the way the beloved wants to be loved.

How can you express love the feminine way? Why feminine? Because it is the feminine energy that integrates, that makes a house a home. Masculine energy is confrontational. It is the hunter that needs to win. So to be loving, to love and be loved, get that cowboy hat off your head. Relax your muscles. Let your heart talk now. How?

Give your time. Time is the scarcest and most valuable asset a human can have. And the biggest, most valuable present we can give is dedicating time to our loved ones.

Take a day off. Spend it with each other. No phones. No appointments. Nothing but being together. Make your loved one feel prioritized. Go hiking. Go to a park, a botanical garden, a museum. Go visit art galleries. Go to the best restaurant in town, just the two of you.

In doing so, you are giving your undivided attention. Because the pace of life has become so hectic, it's imperative to block out time—an evening every week, for instance—for a date with your loved one.

That blocked-out time together, away from work, children, friends, or any attention-grabbing parties, becomes your insurance policy to protect your love against the continuous distractions of modern life.

If you travel a lot, or are employed in a very stressful position, the danger to love is even greater. Thus, your premium should be even higher. A secluded get-together once a week might not be enough. You might have to carve more time out of your schedule, time to be present and loving with those you claim to love. Walk the talk or your marriage might end in all walk and no talk.

Be present. What is the meaning of dedicating your "undivided attention" to love? Have you noticed how at times you may be looking at something but failing to process what you are looking at?

When I was young, I would read all the time, and that included when I was eating. My parents used to yell at me: "When you eat, eat—don't read. When you read, read—don't eat." I could not understand why they were so upset. What was I doing wrong?

Many years later, in meditation and yoga, I was introduced to the concept of "being present." I began to wonder, What does it mean to be present? Now, I understand my parents.

If your mind is not on what you are eating, you will not even know what you are eating. You will not enjoy the food if your mind is somewhere else.

Being present means your mind and body are in the same place at the same time.

Some yogis insist that in order to be integrated, one must not even speak while eating. Be mindful exclusively of what you are chewing and swallowing.

Eliminate temptations that are obstacles to being present.

All kinds of screens—from TV screens to smartphones to tablets—populate our lives everywhere. Even when you go to restaurants to eat, often there are TVs blaring, and you cannot avoid looking up to see what's going on. People eat or drink as they watch screens around them. Screens have invaded homes, too. I have visited families who installed them in their dining rooms so they can watch TV as they eat breakfast, lunch, or dinner.

With smartphones and tablets, people can double- or triple-task simultaneously: eating, speaking on the phone, and watching TV. No wonder people often can't remember what they ate or exactly what they said or were told.

Why is being present so important? Because you must be present to enjoy what you are doing. And that includes love. The more love in your life, the better your quality of life. When your mind is not where your body is, you enjoy life—and love—less.

Feel more, think less. In order to *see*, it is not enough to *look*. You need to be present. Your mind has to be where your eyes are. And to be present, you must stop thinking. Focus on the person in front of you. Notice what they are wearing. Are they happy, sad, angry, or inquisitive? Make eye contact. Feel and do not judge. What prevents you from being present is an active mind that constantly wanders from the past to the future through to the present. And the present is really a mini second between the past and the future. Unless it is present continuous, and that will happen when you stop your mind from wandering from past to future and back. How?

You cannot solve the problem with what is causing the problem.

The villain here is the mind, so asking it to be present will not work. Ask the heart. Feel. When you feel, there is no future nor a past. Only the present. Feel the trees. Their leaves. The clouds. The smell of the roses. Feel the person you are talking to.

Laugh together. The more laughter, the better the quality of life. So focus on subjects that make you both laugh. That, too, will make you feel present. It's impossible to laugh without being present. Your mind must be where you are if anything is going to be funny.

People who laugh cannot have negative thoughts at the same time.

And sing a lot. There is a Montenegrin expression: *Ko peva zlo ne misli.* You cannot sing and have malicious thoughts. Just cannot. When you sing, you love.

PART II

Relationships

The Inevitability of Change and Its Impact

The solution to all problems is love.

Change in the market, in technology—any major change—requires an organization, person, family, or country to adapt or be proactive in responding to the change. Change requires decisions to be made and implemented. The changes "out there" require us to make changes "in here."

But all parts of our system do not change at the same speed. Some change faster than others. Different parts have different lifespans. As we get older, we fall apart just like an old car falls apart with time. The same applies to a company. Marketing changes fast; production slower; accounting, much, much slower. The most difficult challenge is changing people's mindsets and thus their behavior. Same for a country. Technology changes very fast; the economic subsystem is slower to change and is trailed by the legal subsystem. The slowest one to change is the social subsystem, our values, our mindset.

Because of that, the overall system develops cracks. Gaps. It's called disintegration. People are falling apart, which manifests in increasing rates of depression. Families are falling apart, which is reflected in the rate of divorces. And countries are falling apart, too. The disintegration is manifested in what we call "problems".

THE IMPACT OF CHANGE

Whenever there is change, there are problems. When confronted with a problem, people must make decisions. It is like coming to an intersection in a foreign country without GPS or a map. We have to decide: go left, right, back, or stay put, and that includes deciding to do nothing.

Decisions, however, are not enough. Many of us decide to go on a diet but postpone doing it for too long. To manage change, decisions must be implemented.

Success is not just a function of the quality of the decision you make, but also of the efficiency with which you implement it.

As our modern world is experiencing change, the faster the rate of change, the more frequently we must make decisions and implement them. It means handling uncertainties and undertaking risks. The result is STRESS.

People are more stressed now than in the past. Because of technological advancements, our standard of living has gone up. But because of the stress that change generates, our quality of life has gone down. I'd argue our ancestors were poorer and had shorter lifespans, but they were less stressed. Today, in the West, we have a better standard of living but a lower quality of life.

How should we handle change and the problems it generates effectively without the negative repercussions of unhealthy stress?

BE DIFFERENT TOGETHER

Diversity can create synergy.

We are not perfect. Nobody's perfect. But if nobody's perfect, does it mean that the whole world will be badly managed?

What we need to do is work together as a complementary team where we complement each other's weaknesses with our strengths.

Marriage or any committed relationship is a complementary system. We naturally marry someone whose style is different from ours. We fall in love with the strength our partner shows in areas where we are ineffectual. That's why when we introduce a spouse (at least in Western society), we say, "May I introduce you to my better half?" Why are they the better half? Because they are better than we are in areas where we are weak. We are each other's better half, and together we are better off.

This does not apply only to marriage. All systems need to be complementary to be healthy. In a company, the team needs to be complementary. The same principle applies for a country. Diversity is welcomed. Diversity fosters synergy. The differences provide cross-pollinating information which, when exchanged and debated, can create synergy and growth.

However, the question left open is: Why should the diversified elements collaborate and create synergy? What motivates not only collaboration in decision making but also cooperation in implementation?

THE INEVITABILITY OF CONFLICT

Life is a conflict of interests.

To cooperate, there needs to be common interest. If there is no common interest, cooperation will suffer.

But life is a conflict of interests. Within my own body, my brain tells me, "Don't eat that cake! Thirty seconds on your lips, a lifetime on your hips." And my taste buds say, "Eat it, eat it. You deserve it!" You want to sleep, but there is work to do. You want to go on vacation, but you need to budget your money between multiple purposes.

Thus we have two causes of conflict.

Because a complementary team comprises people with different styles, there will be conflict. Some see the big picture; others, the small details. Some think fast. Others take their time.

Another source of conflict arises from the implementation side. In order to implement something, others need to cooperate. You are not operating in a vacuum. You need the cooperation of your neighbors, of the people in your company, of your resource providers. Their interests might differ.

The diversity of styles, cultures, and interests causes conflict. The more change, the more conflict there will be. Take, for example, a family. There's a diversity of styles: One spouse is usually in a hurry to decide, and hates too much discussion and long deliberations. The other wants to understand in depth the issues and will feel ignored. On top of it, there is also a diversity of interests: One of them has interests that are materialistic in nature, and wants maximum financial comfort. The other is interested in spiritual growth and is less interested in money and its benefits.

We think differently and we do not necessarily have common interests. Thus, conflict is a normal, expected phenomenon. The problem is that it can be destructive.

But it does not need to be.

Why did Yugoslavia—a country that does not exist anymore—fall apart? Why did the Soviet Union fall apart? Look at Switzerland; it should be falling apart, too. French people, Italians, and Germans together in one country. That should be a disaster. That country should have fallen apart. But it has not. Analyze marriages. A couple may have conflict, but at the end of the day they love each other more—not in spite of the conflict, but because of it. Another marriage with the same conflict is getting ready for divorce. One is a "Switzerland"; the other is a "Yugoslavia."

What makes the difference?

It all depends upon whether we respect and trust each other or not.

WORK TOWARD "SYMBERGY"

What makes conflict positive in *deciding* is mutual respect: I accept your difference because I can learn from you, and you accept my difference because you can learn from me.

When we learn from each other, uncertainty is reduced and synergy occurs. We make a better decision than we could have made alone.

And on the implementation side, how do we make conflict positive? We are having a conflict of interest: what you want, I don't want. What do we do?

There is an expression, in most languages, that says, "Life is a give and take." We have a conflict of interest, but if it's more important to you, we'll do it your way. Not a big deal. Next time we'll do it my way. It doesn't have to be my way or your way. Give and take.

When I was lecturing in Turkey, an executive approached me and said, "Dr. Adizes, in Turkish, we don't say, 'Give and take.' We say, 'Take and give.'"

There is a difference. Do you first take, or do you first give? When you first give, you trust you will benefit from cooperating and making the system you belong to a better one. If you say, "First I take, then I'll see whether I want to give," there is no trust.

What makes conflict of interest positive is the presence of mutual trust. Do we trust each other? Do we trust that the system we are contributing to will benefit us in return?

If there is mutual trust and respect, there is collaboration in decision making and cooperation in implementation. There is **symb**iosis and syn**ergy**, which I call **SYMBERGY**.

One of my clients, Ricardo Salinas, calls it *prosperidad incluyente*, inclusive prosperity. Prosperity is the result of having synergy, growth. Inclusive means all those who participated in producing this prosperity share in it, thus symbiosis. Synergy (prosperity) without sharing (symbiosis) is short-lived.

What makes America the leader of the free world, the strongest economy on earth? Not size. Other countries are equal in size, if not bigger. Not physical resources. Others have equal or greater resources, too. So what is it?

I believe it is America's culture of live and let live, a culture of mutual respect of differences (ethnic, religious, sexual), and a culture of mutual trust, in the stock market, in the judicial system, in the government. It is far from perfect or even to be praised, but in comparison to other countries it is to be envied.

The biggest assets a person can have are their self-respect and self-trust. Same for a company or a committed relationship: mutual respect and trust are the most valuable assets a company, a marriage, or a country can have.

Energy is fixed at any point in time. We know that from physics theory. The less mutual trust and respect in a system—the more fighting, rumors, and misunderstandings—the more energy is wasted. Think about a situation you had in a relationship, whether in a marriage or at work, where there was no respect and no trust. How much energy did you have when it was over?

As the fixed available energy is depleted, less is available to handle the external environment successfully. Less energy to work that day. Less energy to create. To be productive. And for sure no energy to love.

PROCESS WITH THE HEART

Some radical political parties and radical religions try to stop change. But throughout history, no one has succeeded in stopping change in a sustainable way.

Thus, we must learn to manage change without destructive conflict.

How?

If all problems stem from disintegration, the solution is integration.

What is the ultimate, utmost integration? Love. And love is not sustainable if there is no mutual trust and respect.

And what is love? Love is not give *and* take. You don't take your children to play somewhere, or feed them, because they're going to give back to you. It's not so you can write in your diary: "I took my children to the circus on such and such a day. I gave them something. In the future, I expect them to pay me back and take care of me when I am old and feeble."

Is that why you took them? Life is give *and* take, no?

In the Sephardic tradition, to expect from your children is a curse. You give to your children and should expect nothing in return. So why did you take them to the circus? Because you love them and want them to enjoy the show. And what is your reward? Their joy. You are happy because they are happy.

So, while life is give and take, there is a time gap between giving and taking.

Love is where in the giving is the taking.

It is simultaneous. That is why you should give "with all your heart," without doubting your giving. When it is done from the heart, that is when love is expressed.

In the Jewish tradition, giving should be anonymous so that you expect nothing in return. That is how you practice love—in the giving itself, you find your reward. That is why, in the Buddhist tradition, a Buddhist would say, "Thank you for allowing me to serve you." By giving, they are rewarded.

When you love, you don't think. You don't do accounting; you don't measure the cost/value relationship. "How much am I giving? Am I getting anything back?"

Love is absolute integration. And integration is the solution to a disintegrating society driven by change. Technology is uniting us on one hand, making the world one big village. At the same time, it is breaking us apart socially, politically, emotionally.

So what is the solution to a world that is falling apart?

Love.

Look at the advance of humanity. If you are Darwinian, you know we shared a common ancestor with the chimpanzee. The strongest was the leader. Then we became a nomadic society. The best hunter was the leader. Then we settled, and the person with the most cows or sheep or land was the leader. The common denominator: power and possessions. That was the legitimization for colonialism. The more land, physical resources, and captive markets, the better.

Then came the Industrial Revolution. The brain got into action. Now we had to plan, budget, and organize. In the twenty-first century, we live in a post-industrial society. The brain is now the dominant factor for success. Physical assets play a lower role. Consider Israel, a country that is 60 percent desert and with hardly any physical resources. But it has a tremendous stock of brainpower. Witness how well it has done with its economy. It has the highest number of unicorn companies per capita in the world.

The most valuable companies have few if any physical assets. No muscles. They are mostly, if not entirely, brain.

Uber does not possess a single car. Airbnb has not one hotel. What they have are computers and information and the capability to manage them. Brain.

Some would say that the brain is on its way out as a source of power, too. It is being replaced by artificial intelligence and by quantum computing. So what is next? The soul that supposedly dwells in the heart. The heart should replace the muscle and the brain. And what is this soul? For me, total integration, which is love.

If we as humanity do not develop and nourish our spiritual side, nourish the heart—in other words, love—our future might be like that of Nazi Germany, consisting entirely of power, muscle, and brain but no heart. We will be doomed as a civilization.

Here is a letter that was found at the end of World War II, in a Nazi death camp, that is worth reading twice:

> *What Is Education?*
>
> *Dear Teachers,*
>
> *I am a survivor of a concentration camp. My eyes saw what no man should witness. Gas chambers built by learned engineers. Children poisoned by educated physicians. Infants killed by trained nurses. Women and babies shot and burnt by high school and college graduates. So, I am suspicious of education. My request is: Help your students become human. Your efforts must never produce learned monsters, skilled psychopaths, educated illiterates. Reading, writing, arithmetic are important only if they serve towards making our children more humane.*

We know from research that babies who are not loved do not gain as much weight. Children who grow up in an orphanage or are neglected at home, deprived of parental love, can have serious developmental problems.

We all know from personal experience how lonely and depressing it is not to be in a loving relationship.

It is not the need for affiliation. That need is from your brain, to socialize, to interrelate. It is not the need for sexual release either. That is physical. It is to love with your heart, to ache with your heart to be united with someone whom you feel as one. It is spiritual.

I suggest that even prisoners who have committed violent crimes become more humanized when given a dog to raise. The love that dog gives them changes their behavior better and faster than any talk therapy.

We are trying to solve our life problems with our brains, analyzing cost-benefit ratios.

The real, sustainable solution is processed by the heart, where we feel.

The brain interferes with our need to love or be loved; it has to process all other needs. One of them is fear, which is related to the need to survive. Another is to achieve, and some of us are so busy with our careers that we have no time to feel and love another.

Calm the brain. Think less and let your heart manifest the love it naturally has. Relationships based on love survive.

Communicating Effectively

Less talk, more heartfelt action.

A Molotov[1] cocktail is a bottle filled with two liquids, stoppered, and topped with a lit wick. The combination of these three ingredients—the two liquids and the spark—is explosive. When thrown, the bottle explodes and starts a fire.

Similarly, when a person trying to communicate activates multiple organs in their body at the same time, they can create a dangerous concoction: the person might explode with anger or fury. These organs are the stomach, the brain, and the mouth. They are responsible for feeling, thinking, and speaking, respectively.

[1] Named after Vyacheslav Molotov, Minister of Foreign Affairs for the Soviet Union during the 1940s.

DO NOT BAKE AND SERVE AT THE SAME TIME

Some people speak and think at the same time. They activate two organs simultaneously: the brain and the mouth. They think about what they want to say as they're saying it.

If you have ever encountered a person who does this, you know how confusing they can be. They will repeat themselves and change their message from one minute to the next. They are communicating their own deliberations.

The Serbian expression for combatting this type of communication is *tri put peci, jedanput reci*, which means, "Bake it three times, and say it once." The other universal version of this expression, which comes from measuring cloth when sewing, is "measure twice, cut once."

If you are thinking about what you want to say while you are saying it, you are "cutting the cloth" while measuring it, or before measuring it. You are simultaneously baking and serving the cake. If you activate your mouth and brain together, you will contradict yourself. You will disagree with things you said just minutes before, and then you will get upset with the listener for not understanding you. You might even accuse them of not wanting to understand you.

THE *RIGHT* SEQUENCE

Open your mouth only when your brain is done thinking.

Try calming your brain before opening your mouth and see what happens. I believe you will speak slowly and confidently. Otherwise, you may speak quickly and in broken sentences. The Hebrew expression says, *Divrey hachamim be nahat nishmaeem* ("The messages of wise people are listened to peacefully").

Communication is even worse when the stomach and mouth are activated simultaneously.

A deep message, one that we have not yet articulated, starts in the stomach. We know that we feel something. We are hurt or upset. We feel uncomfortable. Some people even get a stomachache when they need to communicate something *sensitive*, especially if they fear retribution. Some run to the restroom to vomit, or they become indisposed.

If we start speaking before we have clarified what we are upset about, then we are activating the stomach and mouth simultaneously. What will emerge are accusations, offenses, pure feelings, some crying, and—even worse—calls for action. We will find ourselves saying things like, "Let us go our separate ways," and regret what we said later. The message went from feeling to speech without being thought over.

If you are uncomfortable, upset, or emotional—if your stomach is acting up—keep your mouth closed.

Before you communicate the idea, you must calm down your stomach.

Write it all down.

Bring the issues bothering you from the stomach to the brain.

If your write-up is still emotional, keep writing until it is not. Now diagnose what you wrote and see if you can come to a conclusion about what you are thinking.

Once your stomach and brain are quiet, now go, open your mouth, and speak.

HEAR, LISTEN, FEEL

You cannot think and feel at the same time.

Many years ago, I was lecturing in Monterrey, Mexico. At the time, I did not speak modern Spanish. I asked permission to lecture in *Judeo Español*, which is a medieval Spanish language spoken by the Jewish people, who continued to speak it even after they'd been expelled from Spain by the Inquisition 500 years ago. Our family, like many other Sephardic families, spoke it at home. I learned it from my grandmother, who knew no other language.

The organizers agreed.

At a certain point in the lecture, I asked the audience, in this ancient language, if they heard me. I used the word *sentir*. I noticed the audience was uncomfortable. I asked them in English what I had said that confused them. They said: "You asked us if we feel you."

Five hundred years ago the word *sentir* meant "to hear," "listen," and "feel." It meant to sense. Think of a dog. It hears, listens, and feels what is going on, all simultaneously. Modern Latin-based languages—French, Italian, Portuguese, modern Spanish—gave the word *sentir* one of those meanings. In French it is "to smell," in modern Spanish it is "to feel," and in Italian it is "to hear." Modern Spanish still has remnants of the meaning of *sentir* as "to hear": a person who is hard of hearing is *mal de sentido*. A one-way street is *un sentido* (communicating with hard-to-hear people feels like a one-way communication).

My insight is that the ancient person was more integrated. There was one word for hear, listen, feel. When they heard, they listened, and when they listened, they felt what was going on. We now have three words. In modern Spanish, *oir* for "to hear," *escuchar* for "to listen," and *sentir* for "to feel." So today the modern human can hear but not really listen, or can listen but not really feel what is being said. Disjointed. And it all causes problems of communication, especially in intimate relations. As we argue some painful subject, we are so busy feeling, we do not hear. And if we do, we do not listen. The result: a conversation of emotionally deaf people.

In comparison to the past, contemporary life provides a constant avalanche of stimuli. The mind often wanders to something other than what is being communicated. People talk to us and we hear but do not listen. And if we listen, we do not necessarily show empathy and feel what is being told to us.

The modern person is less "together" than the primitive one.

What to do?

To hear, it's only necessary not to be hard of hearing.

To listen, however, requires that you use your mind to focus on what you hear. You must not allow foreign thoughts to distract you from the subject at hand.

Now, what about feeling?

In order to feel, you have to stop processing information, stop trying to understand, so you can *feel. You cannot think and feel at the same time.* Not well, anyway. When you feel, you "read" the words between the lines that are not being said. You interpret the meaning of the message communicated beyond comprehending every word spoken.

To hear, you need not to be distracted by other noises.

To listen, you have to be present and have your mind where your body is.

To feel, you have to stop listening. Stop trying to understand and just FEEL.

Maybe our prolonged formal education makes us more cerebral, less-feeling creatures. We hear and are often forced to listen—but we do not feel.

We know a lot, but understand very little.

PRACTICE EMPATHY

Feelings should be responded to with feelings.

I was once watching a mother soothing her crying child when I realized that very few words were expressed. Hardly any at all. The mother was holding her daughter close to her chest, kissing and caressing her lightly. The only sounds I could hear were soft murmurs of love.

At the end of the day, I thought to myself, all people are children at heart. When we are in pain, all we want is to be loved, caressed, held close to the heart, comforted by someone we love. Not by words. By feeling love.

At moments of hurt and anguish, words only interfere with our need to feel and be felt.

From my observations, women, when in emotional pain, do not seek advice—which if offered unsolicited could lead to anger—but are longing for someone who can sense them, care, and connect to their feelings. What I call "feel to feel."

But, come to think of it, men need and desire the same kind of response. Imagine a man coming home from some interaction that went badly. His partner tries to talk him out of how he feels, tries to use logic, tries to persuade him not to be unhappy. This would probably trigger a predictable response: he would be unfulfilled and frustrated. Like a woman, he too wants emotional support.

Logical issues should be handled with logic, and feelings should be handled with feelings.

Think of a person dying. Imagine someone attempting to reason, explaining that it's all God's will, that there is life after death, and it's probably not so terrible after all. This kind of response to a tragic event is an extreme example of feelings handled with logic, with words. Something else is required. Something simpler, direct. Perhaps as slight a gesture as holding their hand. Silently. With a caress.

Or placing a hand on their heart. Gazing directly at their eyes. It becomes a way of showing love. Of transmitting a sense of caring. No words. Talk will only interfere. It will only blur the connection. That's because feelings should be responded to with feelings.

Notice lovers sitting on a bench by the beach at sunset. Is one saying, "Let me tell you the many ways *why* I love you," or just holding their loved one in an embrace and not saying a word?

Speaking would ruin the moment.

Feelings come from the heart and, yes, there is and can be heart-to-heart communion. Without declaring a sentence or uttering a word.

The mind speaks with words; the heart with feeling transmitted in silence.

By the same token, I feel we should handle logical issues not with feelings, but with logic. Imagine that you ask someone for advice, explaining a situation where something went wrong. Instead of reasoning with you, offering alternate or possible paths to follow, the person tries to hold your hand, hugs you in an effort to offer comfort, and tries to make you feel better. You would most likely dismiss that person in a heartbeat. You were seeking advice, not emotional support, tough analytical reasoning, not sympathy or empathy.

To me, this insight, which evolved as I watched a mother soothe a crying child, has repercussions within marriage, in a lover's fight, and even in a business partnership turning sour.

What hurts people, is not what happens *to them but what it means to them.*

To help someone who is emotionally hurt, we need first to empathize. When the hurt person calms down and asks for our comments—in effect, wants us to speak—only then should we respond with words of understanding. But not sooner.

If this insight makes sense, it has repercussions in international relations as well. For example, today there is still no peace in the Middle East. I suggest that there will be none until both sides are able and willing to respond to each other with "heart speak," not "mind speak," with actions from the heart and not words expressing the mind.

What is happening instead is that words of negotiation have become the form and substance of exchange. They have replaced the feeling side of the equation. What they have left on the table is all barter and logic—rational thinking such as who did what to whom, who is the victim and who is the villain. All the while, the real problem is staring us (and them) in the face: Jewish hearts bleeding from the Holocaust, and Palestinian hearts torn by the loss of home and land.

This is not to suggest that international conflicts get resolved the same way as interpersonal ones, holding hands and looking into one another's eyes. But there are still ways each side can turn to one another with an open heart. Less talk, more heartfelt action.

Here is an example: the organization Physicians for Human Rights in Israel. Every Saturday, dozens of Jewish and Israeli Arab physicians, together, visit a different Palestinian village and offer their medical services free of charge. That seems to me a feel-to-feel act. An action from the heart. Less talk and more acts of love that stimulate the right feelings.

If there is going to be peace in a marriage, in a partnership going sour, in international relations, the path must lead from the heart and include far fewer words. At least to start with.

TRY MIRRORING

It frequently occurs in discussions, when someone does not agree with you, that they will say: "No, you don't understand what I said. You're not listening."

They appear to be claiming that if you disagree with them, it is because you're not listening well and thus you don't understand their argument. This is often not true. You are listening, and you understand what they're saying. You just don't agree.

The other party is intimidating you into agreeing. What to do? It is called "mirroring." Tell the person, "I did listen. Let me repeat what you said and tell me if I missed anything," and repeat the other person's argument quietly without allowing interruption. Now ask the other party to validate that you did hear them and understood their argument well.

After you mirror their argument, what often happens is that they understand their own argument better now that they've heard it from someone else and they will start adding to, or changing, their reasoning. In that case, repeat the mirroring. It might take several attempts to really comprehend what they are saying and make them understand their own argument better.

After they acknowledge that you do understand them, make your counter argument. But not before they grant that you have understood their point well.

This routine to deal with a heated emotional argument or discussion needs strong self-control of one's emotions. Their claim that you do not listen, when in fact you do, can come across to you as an unfair personal criticism. It can be offensive and stir up an emotional response. Relax. Do not take it personally. Just listen and write down their argument. Then break it down into its components so when you mirror, you are crystal clear about what their argument is. And then go and respond.

It does not always work out. I can lose my patience listening to someone who argues nonstop and is repeatedly offensive. To me it feels like they are not trying to exchange points of view so we'll learn from each other, but rather they are arguing to win the debate. And to win the debate, the rules of the game are different from the rules to understand the argument. To win the debate, people are constantly changing their arguments. In that case, I disengage.

Building Relationships That Last

Life lived well is going for the roller-coaster ride without fear, in the hopeful expectation that every down will have its corresponding up, and learning both individually *and* together *from each new change that life presents.*

Years ago, a good friend of mine told me that he was unhappy being single. He wanted a change in his life. The dating process, he said, was emotionally exhausting. The women he spent time with were too shallow. He wanted a woman with intellectual depth. He was impatient. Where was she?

Time passed, and he finally found and married the "right" woman: brilliant, confident, and self-assured.

A few years later, my friend reported unhappiness in his marriage. He needed a change in his life. His wife—the brilliant woman with intellectual depth—was "too cold." She was also "distant" and "insufficiently intimate."

He got a divorce. A year or so later, he got married to a woman who could "express her love," who was "outgoing" and full of a "zest for life." Six months into the marriage, though, unhappiness settled in again.

His new wife was so needy and demanding that he felt suffocated. He, again, sought a change in his life, and once again he was contemplating divorce.

I remember thinking to myself, he's looking for a woman who has no faults. The perfect wife.

And this is a wish we often hear from young people about their search for a "soul mate"—the perfect partner.

THE IDEA OF A SOUL MATE

It reminds me of the title of one of my books: *The Ideal Executive: Why You Cannot Be One and What to Do About It.* By the same token, there is no ideal "soul mate."

Why?

Because there is nothing perfect in this world. And as the situation changes, what sublimely fit the conditions of one moment might not apply moments later. What felt ideal yesterday might feel inappropriate today.

Does this mean we should abandon the endless search for that perfect mate whom we brand as our "soul mate"?

No.

For a sustainable soul mate, a life partner, search for one who seeks to become one.

Allow me to explain.

What are the attributes of a soul mate? Is it someone who is a perfect match? Somebody with whom you will not have any conflict? A person who understands you, and whom you understand fully and effortlessly? In other words, someone who is basically perfect, lacking any weaknesses that could annoy you?

They do not exist.

What you need is a *complementary* person, a not-so-perfect spouse who has your weaknesses as their strengths, so that together you might fully realize the needs of a family.

But there is a catch.

Since we are different and no one is perfect, there is going to be conflict. And as we have seen in previous chapters, because we seek the complementarity and conflict is therefore unavoidable, the key is to make it constructive.

When is this conflict constructive? When there is mutual trust and respect. When there is faith that you two have common interests and there is faith you can each learn from your differences.

I therefore suggest that a soul mate is someone whom you trust and respect, and whose faults you can live with. Someone who shares your interests and from whom you can learn. Through mutual trust and respect, you grow together and, over time, you become better than who you were when the relationship started.

Look for a person you are attracted to, whom you respect and trust, from whom you can learn, and who is willing to learn from you and who shares your values. Over time, that person will develop to be your soul mate.

Life is full of change; a true roller coaster with ups and downs that are often completely unexpected. A soul mate is someone with whom, when the relationship is down, you can hold your breath and learn what you can learn from the experience until the relationship improves. Conversely, when the relationship is up, be prepared for the inevitable moment when things get subjected to the laws of disintegration. In other words, no unnecessary excitement nor unnecessary depression. Love and learn.

Expecting the roller coaster to head forever upward, or coast along on a flat plain, is a recipe for unhappiness. Expecting, instead, to learn from each up or down shift you experience together is a much more realistic, and fulfilling, goal for mature relationships. We "fall in love" because of trait A, B, or C that is possessed by the object of our affection. Mature love means *to love somebody in spite of* faults X, Y, and Z—knowing full well what those faults are and choosing to build our lives around that person anyway.

We like others because *of their strengths, and we love them* in spite of *their weaknesses.*

What is true about relationships, of course, is true in the larger sense about all of life. Life lived well is going for the roller-coaster ride without fear, in the hopeful expectation that every down will have its corresponding up, and learning both *individually* and *together* from each new change that life presents.

THE ROLE OF COMMITMENT

A high level of commitment is required for a relationship or marriage to last and be sustainable throughout its lifecycle. That's why in weddings of the religions I know, the pair is asked if they are committed to each other for good and bad times. They are not asked to commit to love each other. Even the all-powerful God in the Ten Commandments did not instruct us to love. God said to "honor."

In Jewish weddings, the groom stomps on a glass and breaks it apart. Immediately, the orchestra starts playing wedding music, the audience erupts in applause, and everyone starts singing and dancing.

This ritual—typically interpreted as a reminder of the temple's destruction that's not to be forgotten even at times of our highest happiness—may symbolize the *irreversibility of the marriage*, once it's signed, sealed, and delivered. Much in the same way that a glass broken cannot be put back together, marriage is meant to be an irreversible event for which a high commitment is required.

Love without commitment is not sustainable, and marriage without love is not worth having.

WHY BE MARRIED?

Consider marriage from a functional point of view: What does it fulfill? What needs does it satisfy?

Let us start by looking at traditional marriage from a woman's point of view.

In previous times, the role of a woman in society was to devote herself exclusively to raising children and serving her man. She needed a man to conceive and to bring home the financial support necessary so that she could focus on the family. Ideally, he shared the responsibility of parenting by being the disciplinarian. He also provided physical help around the home by fixing, building, moving things, etc., in addition to social status from his place of employment and involvement in the community.

The world has changed.

In the modern world, in developed countries, a woman—at least in the middle class and upper socioeconomic strata—de facto no longer needs a man to satisfy these needs. She can meet these demands herself, or simply outsource them.

She can earn money and social status on her own. To conceive, she can go to a sperm bank and even choose the likelihood of her future child's eye or hair color. If she earns money, her child can have a nanny, go to a day care or nursery school, and when the kid is older, they also can participate in after-school planned activities while she works. A religious leader, the extended family, a good friend, or even a member of a Big Brothers or Big Sisters program can help with the responsibility of parenting. If a woman needs physical help, she can hire a repairperson. If she needs sex, that is also easily available. So, who needs a man in the house making endless demands? More energy is lost than benefits gained.

What about marriage from a man's perspective?

Sex is very easy to find today, and the variety and availability is huge. If a man needs a social partner, many ladies will gladly join him. How about the need to prepare food? A man can cook for himself, eat out, or order meals for delivery. Who will clean the house? He can do it himself or hire a cleaner. He needs a woman to conceive, yes, but even that can be arranged without being married.

So, why marry?

The most valuable asset a company has is what it cannot sell. —David Tice

This phrasing—the most valuable asset is "what you cannot sell"—refers to the company's system of values, but it applies to individuals and can apply to a marriage, too.

What is it that "cannot be sold"—and, by definition, "cannot be bought"? There is one function that cannot be delegated or outsourced, by either man or woman, and that is *love*. Love for each other.

Love cannot be bought or sold. The feeling of deep, real, honest affiliation, of real belonging, cannot be bought or sold anywhere.

All the other reasons for being married, at best, are temporary ones. The kids grow up and leave the house. Money comes and goes. Friends scatter around the globe. What is left at the end of the day? Why be married if there is no more love? Pure love. True love.

And how do we know if it is pure, honest love?

If you are married, remove from your head all the reasons why you are married to your spouse. If you had no children (and no pets you were attached to), and you were broke, or your spouse went broke and stopped being a provider, and there were people to take care of you like a housekeeper or a nurse, would you still be married? If all the reasons disappear, what is left?

All the other reasons for being or getting married are based on *fear.* Marriage should not be a response to fear. It can and should be only entered into because of love. Only love. For which there must be faith.

Love applies to children as well. Why have children? In developing countries, they are a source of income for the family. Or they are the insurance that someone will be a provider and caretaker in old age.

These are also reasons based on fear. Unfortunately, fear is a reality—a completely rational one—within a developing country. But fear is not a reasonable response for a man or woman in a developed country. Not with health insurance and an available retirement system.

As for having children for companionship, in today's open-borders world—especially in the United States—kids scatter over vast geographic areas, so that form of companionship is limited.

So why have kids?

To love and be loved. Period.

THE FAMILY LIFECYCLE

For an enduring relationship, you need to choose a partner who will be able to change as the family's needs change.

Organic systems, people, plants, even stars[1] all are subject to change and thus have a lifecycle. They are born, grow, age, and die. Organizations do, too, from the founding vision and infancy through the challenges of a young company in the Go-Go stage to Adolescence to Prime, and beyond that to the Aging stages.[2] The same applies to marriage. It is an organic system with a lifecycle.[3]

What is expected from a spouse, or a partner, changes along the lifecycle of the marriage or the committed relationship in the same way that the leadership style has to change along the lifecycle of an organization, and the parenting style has to change as the offspring grows, matures, and ages.

When we are single, we may have specific requirements, such as popularity and physical attractiveness. When we start looking for a lifetime partner, the requirements change. Now, the question is: Are they an adequate physical, social, and emotional partner?

When children are born, expectations change again. Is the partner a good parent? Can they set boundaries, provide a good example, impart the correct values, and protect the children so they can grow up emotionally, socially, and physically healthy?

When the kids are grown up and are out of the house, the functions and expectations change once again. Now we need a partner for old

[1] The universe is organic as well. See the new status of cosmology in the following video: https://www.youtube.com/watch?app=desktop&v=HD4WthE414k

[2] Adizes, I. *Managing Corporate Lifecycles: Why and How Organizations Grow, Age, and Die and What To Do About It.* Santa Barbara, CA: Adizes Institute Publications, 2004, store.adizes.com.

[3] Adizes, I. with Yechezkel and Ruth Madanes. *The Power of Opposites.* Santa Barbara, CA: Adizes Institute Publications, 2015, store.adizes.com.

age: someone who knows how to use resources efficiently, who is a good traveling companion, someone with whom we can enjoy both conversation and reading quietly in front of the fireplace.

As the functions needed by the long-term relationship change, the behavior, or style, of the partner has to change as well.

For an enduring relationship, you need to choose a partner who will be able to change as the family's needs change. Can a partner be attractive throughout the life of the family (and that is a long time), and be a good parent, and be someone who is also a great conversationalist to grow old with? Can they remain an attractive and physically fit partner throughout the life of the relationship, as well as being a good provider, and someone you can feel emotionally and socially supported by, as you grow old?

As the life span increases, relationships are supposed to last for thirty, forty, and even fifty years. That is a lot of years during which what is needed from a partner will change. The question is: Can the partner change? Does the partner have the necessary qualities to make that change?

THE INSTITUTION OF MARRIAGE

Marriage is considered an "institution." It is not called an "arrangement" or just a "system" or an "organization."

What does the word *institution* mean? It means that there are clear rules of conduct—who does what, when, how, and who is responsible for what—to be followed and respected.

That is how the institution of marriage was run for generations: there were rules of conduct transmitted from one generation to the other, culturally, as to what is the role of the mother, that of the father, that of the firstborn, and that of the last-born, and the role of the grandparents.

I come from a traditional Sephardic culture. My grandmother knew perfectly well what her role was. It was clearly homemaking, making a house into a home, raising children, and taking care of her husband to the point that she would eat before he got home so that she would be available to serve[4] him when he had dinner. She did not rebel against it, to the best of my memory. She was proud of the quality of life she established at home, the quality and behavior of the children, and the happiness of her spouse.

The husband, in turn, was responsible for bringing the money to the house and for fighting the world out there, so the family would have the resources to survive. He was the breadwinner. He was happy if she was happy. A simple world.

If you were to apply today's business terminology, everyone in the family of the simple traditional world had a "measurable" key performance indicator, or KPI. The mother would be appraised by how well the children performed at school and how well behaved they were, the quality of the cooking, and the cleanliness and order that existed in the house. The table, with all the food she cooked, and the children were her portfolio, presented to the family for evaluation.

The father was appraised by how good he was as a provider and as a backup system to discipline the children when the mother failed to get the desired behavior.

The grandparents provided the (I) Integration, monitoring that the husband, the wife, and anyone else in the extended family did not deviate from the norm. They were the judges of the adequacy of behavior and, in a sense, acted as the family's psychotherapists.

[4] The word *serve* is used here consciously, to emphasize the transformation our societies went through in less than a century.

This was how my home was run when my grandparents were alive. This is how I remember the institution of marriage, of having a family—but that was more than eighty years ago.

One can still find such marriages in very traditional or religious families in the Jewish community or in developing countries.

It has all changed in the developed world. With two-career families, with grandparents living far away, with the advance of ready-made food and the culture of eating out, the rituals, the rules of behavior, the expectations—indeed, everything—has changed.

Who is responsible for what, and who is expected to do what, has become unclear. The family institution is in stress. There might be a solution. We cannot rely on tradition transmitted from one generation to the other. We have to make our own rules now.

COMMITTING TO A LIVING DOCUMENT

That means that before getting married or entering a committed relationship, the couple in love should take the time to cool their heads, sit down, and write down their agreement on virtually everything:

- What are the values they hold dear and that will not be violated?
- Who will be responsible for the family's income? One of them or both?
- Who will manage the family's finances?
- Are they hoping to have kids? If so, how many?
- Will either one of them stay at home to raise the children? If not, who will supervise the person who does?
- Where will they live and what house size are they aiming for?
- Who is responsible for what household chores?
- Who manages the kids' school drop-off and pickup?
- How often will they have sexual relations?
- Is it going to be an open relationship or not?

Everything should be discussed openly so that neither one of the party later starts resenting living in an institution in which they did not agree to its rules of conduct. They should discuss and agree on all the details that, if not articulated up front, can be a source of hard feelings later.

This agreement should be up for review on a predetermined date annually, rather than waiting until there is a crisis to review it. Needs change. Expectations change. So, the agreement might need to change, too. But it should be on a predetermined date and thus be handled proactively.

A marriage needs significant love, granted, otherwise why be married—and the more love there is, the fewer rules and policies it will need. But having no agreed up-front processes whatsoever and relying only on love can cost both parties dearly—both emotionally and financially—if and when they get divorced. And if the couple does not get divorced, both parties will be robbed of energy by having endless arguments or hard feelings because their expectations of what the other should or should not do are not being met.

"But it is very unromantic to have such a meeting and such a discussion, and then maybe even a written document," one person told me.

Do all your divorcing before getting married.

BLOCK TIME

Resting the brain allows the heart to open up.

Earlier in the book, in the "How to Love" section, I talked about the importance of blocking special time slots as a way to express love to your partner. It's important to block time to integrate the whole family as well.

Why is this important? Because we live in a culture that emphasizes continuous *doing* and insists that the secret to success is the tireless dedication to, and pursuit of, a goal.

Is there a place for non-doing? Is there value in doing nothing?

There are three pillars of health: eating right, exercising regularly, and sleeping well.

I understand the importance of eating right. If I eat poorly, toxic junk food will damage my body. It makes sense. Similarly, we need exercise. Without regular exercise, your muscles atrophy; you age prematurely, weaken, and become prone to illness. Sleeping sounds like doing nothing. How does it fit into health? Interestingly, the most important posture in yoga is śavāsana—the Corpse Pose. It forces you to lie down and do nothing.

Let's analyze this question with the Adizes methodology and review its formula of success: *Success is the function of external integration divided by internal disintegration.*

You try to succeed in your career, and in whatever you are passionate about, out in the world. The more successful you are externally, the greater the chances that you are unsuccessful internally, in your personal life. When you devote your energy to work, work around the clock, every day of the week, what happens then? No energy for yourself, for the family. The worst-case scenario: Your family falls apart. Your marriage falls apart. You fall apart physically, emotionally, and probably socially.

So, what should you do? Find a balance that works for you. Consider not dedicating your limited energy to external success to the point that you are falling apart internally. At the same time, don't focus exclusively on the internal environment and ignore the external one.

We all need a balanced lifestyle, and the same concept applies to a company.

What, then, is the benefit of doing nothing?

During the day, you're integrating externally. You're working, serving, and handling the environment in which you live. When night comes, what will you be doing? Integrating and reintegrating. How? By having a good night's deep sleep. That's why you wake up in the morning refreshed. Try not to sleep for a week. It is so unhealthy that people collapse. Why? Because you are only doing external integration with no internal re-integration.

In 1974, Harvard Medical School professor Dr. Herbert Benson wrote an article in *Harvard Business Review* advocating for businesspeople to take regular breaks from work to do nothing. Just close your eyes, relax your muscles, and breathe to elicit what he calls the relaxation response. Reintegrate. Start working again. So, it's not only sleep that is necessary. You need to take a pause. This is why we have breaks between classes at school.

People often wait to apply this principle until a crisis in either the internal or external front appears, but then they may unhealthily react and switch between the two. For example, a person may be building a career with no attention to family. Then, a crisis emerges in the family and the person stops everything related to work to deal with it. It may cause them now to lose their job, prompting a career crisis, which takes them away from the family again. One has to, as the idiom says, "chew gum and cross the street at the same time."

How? Program your breaks. Make a habit of taking a pause. Take off one day a week from work. For Christians, it's Sunday. For Muslims, it's Friday. If you're Jewish, it's Sabbath. If you are agnostic, Thursday is available.

We learn about the value of a Sabbath from the Bible.

On the seventh day of creation, God rested.

God, the most powerful entity, and the creator of everything, got tired. He needed rest.

Who among us is more powerful than God and does not need to rest?

But what exactly is it that needs to rest? It is not only the muscles of the hands or legs. The brain, although it is not a muscle physiologically, behaves like a muscle. Use it or lose it. The muscle of the brain needs rest the most. Most of the calories we get from eating go toward making the brain work. In the process of being used, it gets tired.

During the day, the brain works hard. During the night, it recuperates. There is a reason, then, why all living systems sleep. Horses, fishes, and trees sleep. We all do. One of the benefits of meditation during the day is to take a break. You must let the brain rest, or you will make decisions based on bad judgment. The data that must be processed needs more energy than your exhausted brain can provide.

On the Sabbath, religious Jewish people do not work. This includes driving, cooking, and even turning the lights on or off. Years ago, each of these activities required a lot of work. For travel, you had to harness the horse and prepare the chariot. To cook, or to turn on a light, was work because you had to make a fire. Today what consumes our energy is not the horse and the chariot, nor making a fire to turn on the light or to cook. What exhausts the brain is the tsunami of information that comes through the phone and the media, and we should not ignore the human energy that Internet applications consume.

A Jewish person who obeys God's prescriptions to rest on the Sabbath does not carry money in his pocket. Does not do business. Does not negotiate. Will not take or make a phone call. Will not turn on the radio or TV, nor even read the newspaper. On Sabbath, on our resting day, they make time to go to the place of prayer, hug people there, and wish them, "Shabbat shalom." Shalom means peace, to offer peace as a blessing. They take their children and be with them that day of the week—not dealing with problems but connecting with one another and God through prayer. They start the Shabbat on Friday evening with a festive Shabbat dinner attended by all family members and spend it singing Shabbat songs.

You can do this without waiting for God or a religion to order you to. You decide: No phones, no computers. No TV. No radio, nothing that modern life offers that takes energy, on one day of your choice—every week.

When you rest, you open your heart; you can integrate yourself with your family and your community. Realize you are not the center of the universe. You are only a part of it.

Together and in peace.

The Sabbath was the greatest present God gave mankind.

And only to humans. None of the other living entities have it.

A CULTURE OF GIVING

Who gets the most might give the least.

I've made the above observation, which has been substantiated over the years by events I've witnessed.

A friend of mine shared a problem he has with one of his brothers. The middle brother was always very sick when he was young. Their mother worried endlessly about him surviving. She gave all her attention to this child at the expense of the other two. This middle brother grew up to be a very successful businessman and, of the three, he is the wealthiest. But when the time comes to support the parents, he always has an excuse for why he cannot do much.

This is an example, but not a lone one. In my experience it repeats itself many times.

Children learn: Do they only take, or do they have to give, too?

If children are not raised to clean their rooms, fold their laundry, or help prepare their own meals, when they grow up they may need special care all their life. They may expect preferential treatment as an adult, even when it is not available or affordable. Thus, it is important that children be given assignments around the house and taught that they must contribute, whatever their capability, depending on their age. They must learn to give, and not only to take.

And the giving should not stop at the boundaries of the family.

In the Jewish tradition, donation boxes are typically found in the house so that children can regularly put some money into them to plant trees in Israel and redeem the desert. Kids need to learn to give from an early age and see the value in such contributions if they are going to become productive members of society.

I have noticed that generosity and wealth are not necessarily correlated. Some very wealthy people are stingy, and some relatively poor people are generous. That's because generosity is one particular form of expressing love that needs to be developed. It needs to be exercised.

To love and to give is not an inherited trait but a learned habit.

People generally develop good or bad habits from home at an early age, and there is a certain number of years available for every parent to instill these habits. After that, we need to learn to let our children go.

When is that time?

WHEN TO STOP PARENTING

What I'm learning in old age is that at a certain point in time, children resent being parented. They don't want to be told what to do, nor do they want any advice; they don't want to learn from the experience of the elders.

That was not true when I was growing up in the last century. My grandfather's word was the law, including for my father, who was in his forties. My father was also the dominant figure in my family, and I never dared to disobey him. He continued giving me advice and instructions until he died. I didn't like it, but I listened. Yes, it was in the last century. I was born in 1937.

Today, it's a different world. The children become "adults" early. They know the computer technology better than we do. I could not operate the latest TV screens without them. I am constantly asking for help with the latest changes to my computer applications. Now I am the ignorant student, while they are the knowledgeable teacher. They're influenced by TV, social media, external factors, school, their friends. The impact of the family and its control over their behavior has diminished considerably. Thus, they rebel earlier. If you try to control them, they simply run away. You can see that especially in America, where the children, upon high-school graduation, go to college as far away from home as they can. They find jobs far away, too. They want to be independent. Parents who attempt to continue parenting them trigger their resentment and further distancing.

We need to learn to cut the cord and let them go their way. Unless you are asked for advice, don't offer it; let it be.

An interesting analogy is the succession planning in a company. Starting a company is like having a child. The founder loves their company and spends more time building it than they spend with their own children. The day comes when the company is big enough to have good managers beyond the founder, and they, too, want to exercise authority and lead. Can the founder let go and let them make mistakes, or do they continue to "parent," continue to make all the decisions?

If it's the latter, what happens? Like with children, the good managers leave and the weak ones stay, accepting the stage of disempowerment they are in. The company will grow only while the founder is still fully active. When they die, the company eventually will die, too, because no competent successor is available to take over and lead.

We all, in all situations, should know when to let go, or we become the prisoners of our wish to control.

HONORING YOUR PARENTS

How can we reconcile this principle of honoring your parents that is taught in the Bible—and respecting our elders, as many cultures teach—with the fact that, in this time of accelerating change, now the young, who are "technological natives," seem to know more than their elders, act as their teachers/trainers, and refuse to get their advice?

The Hebrew language has two different words denoting respect. One means, literally, "honor," and the other means "value." Honor is how you behave—not what you think. Value is what you think.

In Hebrew, the word *kavod* (honor) comes from the word *kaved* (heavy). To honor means to recognize someone's "weight," or substance. For example, when a person loses their honor, it is as if they've lost weight, but not physically; it is more like losing their good will. A dishonorable person is one who does not keep their word. It is as if they have no anchor to hold their ship in place, nothing to hold onto. They are too light. You cannot rely on such a person. When a family defends its honor, it is defending its brand name, its good will, its assets in the society.

So, what does it mean to "honor your parents"? It means to recognize the assets (opportunities) they are giving you. You did not start from zero. You belong to a group, a system. They gave you something. You are the continuation of that something. You are starting where they are ending. So, can you recognize that and be thankful? That is why you bow and hold your palms together when you honor. You are acknowledging and thanking them for what you've received. The same applies to teachers.

Teachers and parents "teach" you, which you may interpret as them trying to "change" you, and that is painful. It is tough to accept pain and still value it.

Thus, the Bible does not ask us to value our parents. It commands us to behave in a certain way: to honor our parents and teachers regardless of what we think. Whether we value them or not, we should behave as if we do.

In the Adizes methodology, we insist that people behave as if they respect each other even if, in fact, they do not value each other's contributions. You do not know what value people give you until the discussion is over, and even then, it is not clear who is right. But if you honor them, you might learn something.

Why does not the Bible say: "Love your parents"?

Because love is a phenomenon of being totally integrated. Total integration is an utopian expectation. It cannot happen ongoingly forever when there is change, and change was there, is here, and will be forever. So total integration, total love, cannot be forever. Notice, God does not order us to do what cannot be done. No one—not even God—can make you love anyone or keep loving anyone forever. But you can honor them.

Behave honorably—at all times and in all cases. Do not prejudge whether others deserve it or not. Bismarck, the first German chancellor, said, "Respectfully, even to the gallows!"

Threats To Relationships

People do not change but they can improve.

Building and maintaining healthy relationships that are gratifying is not automatic and should not be taken for granted. Continuous change and problems generated by change challenge healthy relationships. It's imperative, thus, to know what are the threats and how to handle them in order to maintain a relationship worth having.

FEAR OR LACK OF TRUST

How did it happen that in the Bible's narrative, the prophet Daniel walked into the lion's cage and the lion didn't kill him? Did God prevent the lion from attacking, or was it Daniel who did something to prevent the attack?

My insight: Daniel believed in God with all his soul and trusted that God would protect him. Believing in God means to me that he was totally relaxed. Trusting. Loving.

There was no signed agreement between God and Daniel. Daniel simply trusted God, and because of that, he felt no fear. When you feel no fear, you do not project to your opponent that you might attack proactively to defend yourself. If you do not intend aggression, there is no need for the other party—in this case the lion—to attack you in its defense.

I learned this while on a walking safari in Africa many years ago. We walked through the reserve without guns or any other protection. I admit I was scared that we might be attacked. There were lions; there were wild animals left and right. The guide calmed us by explaining that every animal has a perimeter within which that animal feels secure, and as long as you do not cross that boundary, they do no harm. If animals don't feel threatened by us, they won't attack us.

I personally took that advice cautiously, calculating that if an animal like a lion is hungry, its radius will probably grow much bigger. The fact, however, is that we walked that safari for days and nothing dangerous happened.

This has applications for personal life and married life. An argument happens, and one of the partners in the marriage raises their voice or doesn't show enough positive attention. In this case he was not attacking. He was just annoyed at something. The other partner misinterprets the first partner's behavior and fears that he is unloved and unappreciated, and will attack. Escalation. Bigger attacks yield bigger fears, which provoke multiple attacks, which result in more and more mutual aggression, and the result could be a separation or a divorce. A big crisis because of misunderstandings. Do not assume. Always validate. In the meantime have no fear. Assume all will turn right until absolutely proven wrong. With facts. Not assumptions.

EXPECTING YOUR PARTNER TO CHANGE

We are what we are.

How many divorces happen because one or both parties insist that the other party must change their personality or style?

People do not change. They can improve. But change the essence? No. We are what we are. It is genetically determined. I was told that research was done in Denmark that followed babies from birth for twenty years to see if their (PAEI) personality style could be determined from an early age.[1]

The researchers concluded that it could be.

(P) babies are in most cases busy looking at what is in front of them. They will pick up your glasses and study them. (A) babies usually do not smile. They watch you closely. They cry if you insist on getting too close. The (E) baby does not even look at you. They are looking around at everything else, jumping from one point of interest to the next. The (I) baby is ready to move to your hands and smiles easily.

Babies, like adults, do not have "one-track" personalities. They have all PAEI traits. To analyze their personalities, watch how they behave most of the time.

Doctor Elliot Abravanel[2] claims his classification of personalities—which corresponds well to the PAEI model of peoples' styles—is driven by different glands: (P) by the adrenal gland, (A) by the pituitary gland,

[1] PAEI is a model I developed to describe management styles. The acronym stands for producer (task-oriented person), administrator (systems, order-oriented style), entrepreneur (creative risk-taker style), integrator (people-oriented style). See Adizes, I. *Management/Mismanagement Styles: How to Identify a Style and What to Do About It.* Santa Barbara, CA: Adizes Institute Publications, 2004, publications.adizes.com.

[2] Abravanel, E. *Dr. Abravanel's Body Type Diet and Lifetime Nutrition Plan.* New York: Bantam Books, 1999 (revised ed.).

(E) by the thyroid gland, and (I) by the hypothalamus's secretion of dopamine. We are born with different levels of activity in each gland. These levels do not drastically change during our lifetimes, and thus neither do our personalities.

We can improve. We can learn. It is essential if we want to communicate and work together, and to relate better to people who are different from us. But we cannot change the essence of who we are.

Now, the question is: What does one do with a person who refuses to learn, refuses to improve? They stick to their style and ignore the repercussions it has on the relationship.

You give them a chance to learn, to grow. If they refuse to improve and their style is destructive, go your separate ways.

The Adizes Institute does not try to change people's leadership style—make an Entrepreneur or Producer into an Integrator, for instance. We are dedicated to style enrichment, not style change. "Enrichment" means to improve the PAEI parts of the personality that are dysfunctional and interfere with teamwork, or the needs of the team.

We have to recognize that people are who they are. The only question that remains is: Can we work with them or not, and what parts of their style must improve to reach the desired teamwork behavior?

SCREAMING VERSUS HITTING

Physical violence is a crime and should be punished. No one should suffer from violence.

When women get married out of love, it must be devastating—spiritually, emotionally, not to mention physically—to be attacked by the person they used to love or maybe still love.

When I was in high school, I volunteered to teach Israeli folk songs and dances to teenage girls in prison. Most were serving sentences for prostitution. I have seen what physical abuse can do to a woman. More so than to a man. Men fight; they face physical confrontations without much contemplation. Not women, in my observations. They are sensitive, and physical confrontation is not in their usual repertoire.

But women know how to be abusive, too. Differently. They might scream at their spouse, put them down, or call them names.

This is extremely painful to men, who seek respect. Granted, both genders need and seek love and respect; it's the ratio I am referring to. I believe, for women, love is the first need. Men, on the other hand, first of all want respect.

For a man, being screamed at, put down, shamed, or criticized for real or imaginary failures is tantamount to being physically hit.

In this case, there are no external signs, no black eyes or blue arms. The injuries are inside the man's soul. They feel beaten and wounded to the core. The woman they married out of love is now rejecting them. It hurts, enormously, often no less than physical abuse.

WORK AND LIFE IMBALANCE

In my lectures and my book *Managing Corporate Lifecycles*,[3] I analyze what happens to a woman who has a newborn. The baby takes all the energy. Feed, change diapers, rock to sleep; the mother gets exhausted. Some have postpartum depression. Some husbands do not read the situation appropriately, and often complain about it and want more time from the partner than they can offer.

[3] Adizes, *Managing Corporate Lifecycles.*

All over the world, having lectured in fifty-two countries, I ask the same question: If the pressures of the husband persist, whom would the wife give up? The husband or the baby? The answer unanimously is she gives up the husband and keeps the baby.

Something similar happens with founders of companies.

My experience with founders of companies is that the start-up company is a sort of a child they have given birth to.

Founders of companies had a period of "pregnancy," when they were dreaming about what they would do. Then they took the plunge, quit their job, took a loan, and "gave birth" to a company. And that "baby"—their start-up—had lots of problems, like all newborns have. Cash-flow problems, inventory problems, quality problems. When the founder comes home exhausted and their spouse expects variety and the enjoyment of "together time," the founder lacks the energy to respond. Then their spouse starts to complain that ever since the founder started the company, they have no family life anymore, and so on.

The spouse misreads the situation, seeing the company as competition, not as a child their loved one has given birth to.

If the spouse continues to put pressure on the founder, and the founder of the company has a choice—the spouse or the company—what does the founder choose?

They often choose the company, their baby.

In companies, I recommend that the spouse be involved so the company is not just run by one spouse, but both. The same applies when the baby is born. Both parents should be involved. *Our* business, *our* baby.

OBSTACLES TO SELF-ACTUALIZATION

I remember being invited to dinner at the home of a CEO with a very traditional family. When we rang the bell, the CEO's wife opened the door. She stood ready to greet him along with their two small children, who were nicely dressed, their faces washed and their hair combed. She kissed her husband, greeted me, and proceeded to present the kids to her husband, telling him how wonderful they were that day. It reminded me of an executive presenting her achievements to her partner.

I remember my mother. Her undisputed empire was the kitchen, and she took pride in the table she set for her guests and the food she had prepared, sometimes working on it for days. That was her "portfolio," and the guests and family appreciated her labor. "*Bendichas manus*" ("Blessed are the hands who cooked all this"), we told her at every meal. "*Bendichas bokas*" ("Blessed are the mouths that eat it"), she would graciously reply.

One day, soon after I arrived in America, I was invited to a dinner. There was smoked salmon for the main course, and a great cake for dessert. I started to congratulate the lady of the house, telling her how wonderful her cooking and baking were, blessing her hands for preparing it . . . and then I stopped, because the guest next to me at the table was nudging me in the ribs with his elbow. He later explained why he'd stopped me from praising the hostess. "Because she didn't cook any of it. You were embarrassing her. In America, we buy it all."

While in a traditional family, taking care of the family was the primary source of self-actualization for the woman, and bringing the bread, that of the man, the boundaries are fuzzy now. For a healthy relationship in the modern family, those responsibilities should be shared and equally appreciated.

Healthy Relationships

Be patient. Practice tolerance. Give space.

As we have said many times already, change challenges relationships. Decisions need to be made and people have different decision-making modes and different interests. How to maintain healthy relationships is a challenge we all face.

TAKING OWNERSHIP OF PROBLEMS

Reframe the problem into what you can control.

Assume you have a spouse or partner who has some attitude problems, such as being overly defensive. And it's troubling you greatly. It is your problem *if* you can make them change their behavior or mental state. If you conclude that you aren't going to change their attitude or behavior, that there is nothing you can do about it, you have to reframe the problem. It has to be reframed into what *you* can do about it. Supposedly you have control over what you think and do. So, now it is your problem, not theirs. You have the problem to decide what to do. Since they are not going to, you have to.

When your spouse or a friend or even someone you don't know very well acts inappropriately, if you cannot control their behavior why are you getting upset? You cannot change them. Why is their problem—their having an attitude—your problem? Who has a problem, whose problem is it, who can do something about it? Who can make a change? Who can solve it?

Reflect on what you can control. Do you want to live with them, or do you not want to live with them anymore? Do you want to be married to this person or not? Do you want to socialize with this person or not? Do you want to be in the same room with this person or not?

Your problems are those you can control or do something about. All the others are facts of life.

Here is a Jewish joke that manifests what I am saying here:

Abe is trying to fall asleep, but it is not working very well. He's tossing and turning in bed.

"What's going on, Abe? Why can't you sleep?" his wife asks him.

"I owe $10,000 to Moish, and I don't have the money to pay him back."

"One moment," she says. She goes to the phone, calls up Moish, and says: "Moish, you remember that Abe owes you $10,000?"

"Yes."

"Well, I'm sorry to tell you, but right now he has no money to pay you back. I'm really sorry."

And she hangs up. Abe is in shock. He looks at her and says, "What the hell did you do that for?"

She says, "Now it is his headache."

Whose problem is it? Whoever can do something about the problem. If Abe cannot do anything about this $10,000, if there's simply nothing he can do, it is not his problem anymore. What he can control now is what to do about his guilt. How he can make amends. The debt is now Moish's problem because he's not going to be paid, at least not now, and he is the one who can do something about it.

We often take other people's problems to be our problem. Because we believe we can make a difference and solve their problem. It is legitimate to try, but when you realize that it is a lost cause, that you cannot make a difference, it is not your problem anymore.

Let us apply this thesis to what we see on TV.

People demonstrate against Israel's occupation and treatment of the Palestinians. Why don't you see any—and I mean *any*—demonstrations against the leader of Syria, who is killing his people indiscriminately? Or of the ethnic cleansings in Africa?

One often repeated explanation is anti-Semitism. Another possible explanation is that people will spend energy, in this case, demonstrate, if they believe there is a chance their demonstration will have an impact and the entity demonstrated against is going to do something about its behavior.

People believe Israel is a democratic society and thus will yield to public opinion. That's why there are demonstrations and negative media. There is no use to demonstrate and spend energy on Al Bashar, the Syrian leader. Such action has zero chance of impacting his behavior, so why waste energy?

Assume a member of the family is an alcoholic. If you can convince them to get treatment and they do, it is their problem because they are taking charge of it. If, on the other hand, they refuse to receive treatment, now the problem is not them—it's you. You have the problem. You cannot influence them to take control of themselves, but you can control yourself. It's your problem now to decide if you want to remain in the relationship or not.

TREATING THE LINES THAT CONNECT THE DOTS

A relationship is more than the sum of its parts.

There have been times in my consulting practice when I've brought in a psychologist to help me. I am trained in management, and the problem was more psychological. I found, to my surprise, that instead of helping, the psychologist was undermining my efforts.

For instance, one client told me: "I told the psychologist that in this company, everyone builds their own army, and we fight a lot. 'Then build your own army,' he said."

After some thought, it occurred to me why the psychologist reacted the way he did. A psychologist focuses on the individual—on their mental health and ability to cope and solve their own problems. The assumption is that if the individual is mentally healthy and functioning, the system—which is composed of multiple such individuals—will function well, too. The rationale is that if the components are no good, the system won't work. What is required for the system to work, therefore, is healing of the components.

A system is more than the sum of its parts. There are interactions that need to be dealt with.

You can have a situation in which all the parties are mentally healthy and yet the system does not work, as happens in some marriages. For instance, the partners may differ in their expectations of what each of them should be responsible for. Each of them is well and stable. It is their interactions that do not work.

The psychologist and I developed our therapies out of different assumptions.

The psychologist's focus is on the component, believing that if the components are healthy, the system will be healthy. My focus with organizational therapy, which I often still call consulting so as not to scare people, is on the system. I believe that if the system works well, the happiness and behavior of each individual in that system will improve.

Recently I came to the realization that treating the system in which the individuals interact applies to marriage counseling as well.[1] They should not treat the dot. They should focus on the lines that connect the dots.

PLAYING THE TEACHER AND THE STUDENT

Disagreements and conflicts are an opportunity to learn, enrich, and support each other.

A lot can be learned through marriage and the resolution of its interpersonal, stylistic issues.

One learns to be patient—from waiting for the spouse to finish dressing and be ready to leave the house, to waiting for the husband to stop watching the football game.

One learns tolerance, and to sometimes accept what one does not like because the other person does like it.

You learn to let your spouse drive in circles, refusing to listen to your instructions, although you know the direction perfectly well. Be patient. Practice tolerance. Give them space.

[1] Adizes et al., *The Power of Opposites.*

You learn to not react when the spouse gets angry. To swallow pride and deal with the issue when "the storm is over."

You learn how to deal with a spouse who at times behaves in an immature manner, and all they may care for at times is just food, drink, sex, and comfort.

One learns to deal with a hurt ego.

Yes, marriage is an ongoing education, and you are being tested in real time, all the time, if you learned your lessons.

It has stern teachers.

Each partner in a marriage is a teacher to the other. We are students and teachers at the same time.

Some do not make it. They flunk the tests and repeat the class over and over. They remarry multiple times, looking for the perfect spouse,[2] a class where there is no conflict and thus nothing to learn anymore. Or they drop the class—in the "marriage university"—altogether and get divorced. Real learning comes with the pain of solving real issues in real time with real people.

You can graduate from a class—for instance, you have learned your lesson on a certain topic—but school continues. Along the way you'll get enrolled, whether you like it or not, in a new class. New conflict. New problems.

You graduate from this school when the classes are review classes. You've learned your lesson, learned what can and cannot be changed, and learned to live with what cannot be changed.

In marriage, as in life, real success depends on how advantageously you handle your failures.

[2] See earlier discussion on "the perfect soul mate."

Marriage success is not how rarely you fall. It is how quickly you get up. Getting up means that each problem, each failure, is an invitation to learn something you did not know before.

The more you learn from mistakes, the wiser you become. The wiser you become, the fewer mistakes you will repeat.

A fool who thinks they are wise is the ignorant one; a wise person who thinks they are ignorant is the wise one.

Thinking you are wise, and know everything you need to know, is what makes you an ignoramus. A person who admits they are ignorant and is constantly learning is the wise person. And how do you really learn? By experience—and that means not being afraid to make mistakes, as long as you learn from them.

Interestingly, not all people suffer in class. There are those who enjoy the learning. The growing. They love to learn and to teach, and love to enrich each other.

When does that happen? When there is mutual trust and respect.

When that happens, disagreements and conflicts are an opportunity to learn, enrich, and support each other.

When that is the case, spouses do not take their conflicts personally. They realize: Here is another opportunity for me to grow up and learn something new.

Without mutual trust and respect, learning is painful. With it, it is invigorating and enriching.

KEEPING THE PERSONAL PRIVATE

As the leader of the Adizes Institute, I insist that there are no secrets, save for proprietary information pertaining to our clients that are sacred. What happens inside the Institute has to be totally transparent. This means if person A comes to me and tells me something about person B (perhaps something has happened that should not have happened), or A has some criticism of B, which they put in an email, I immediately forward that email to B to let them know what A said about them.

This usually gets A very upset with me. They accuse me of being untrustworthy. It is part of my philosophy that if B has a problem with A, or vice versa, they should talk to each other and deal with the issue head on. When A sends me a complaint about B and wants me to keep it a secret, what this really tells me is that the issue is not going to be solved. A is just passing the buck to me about the problem, which frees them from dealing with it. Now I have to deal with B myself while keeping secret that A is the source of the information.

This behavior is toxic and it can often plague a marriage and a family as well. Family members who operate in this fashion can become toxic. They spread rumors and information that cannot be substantiated because they're "secret."

Secrets should be kept sacred when making them public does not bring any benefit, such as when disclosure does not help to solve the secret problem. Take private and personal information, for example. Let's say your friend has cancer. If they want to keep this information private and ask that you not share it with anyone, then you're obliged to not spread it. Spreading your friend's personal information will not help their cancer; it may make people pity them, which will increase their anguish.

So, when you are the keeper of any type of information—the confidant—ask yourself this question: Should this information be kept secret? The answer lies in what can be done about it. If something can be done that requires the cooperation of others, then the information should not be kept secret. If the information (if it were to be revealed) could not be controlled, or if it is solvable only by the individual with, or from whom, it was confided, then it is private. In that case, if the originator asks that it be kept secret, the request should be respected and followed.

TENDING THE GARDEN

One honeymoon is not enough for a lifetime of marriage.

Build the most beautiful garden money can buy. Do not maintain it, and it will be destroyed over time, overflowing with weeds.

Buy the best, most expensive car you can. Do not maintain your car. Do not drive it. Do nothing to it and, in two years, it will not start.

Entropy is natural. With change, things can fall apart. If you don't address it, ruin sets in. What this means is that it is possible to predict failure—in marriage, in business, in our personal lives, and in practically anything we do.

To predict failures just take things for granted. Do nothing.

What happens when you take the love of your spouse for granted? Take your children for granted? Take your employment, your success, your health—take it all for granted and thus do nothing about it. Why should you, you think to yourself, all is well. Be ready for a surprise. Failure will follow.

When we take things for granted, we assume that we can rest and have nothing more to do because we have achieved what we want. So nothing more to do. We take for granted that the situation will not change. And we stick to that belief for a reason.

Adapting to change, and constantly working to maintain success, takes energy. Sometimes, it is very frustrating. To assume that all is fine and will be fine, that there is nothing more to do, is comforting.

Doing nothing does not require energy and we all want to conserve energy.

What will undermine our "success," however, is *change*. Situations change. What was right and made us happy in the past does not always apply in the present—and even if it does, it may not remain as such in the future.

When achieving a goal means we have nothing more to do,

when we take success for granted,

we are writing ourselves a prescription for future failure.

Change will do it.

At the onset of a relationship, you worked hard to earn the love of the one you desired. You did not take love for granted. But some of us, once we were married and got the love we wanted, took that love for granted from then on. We believed love would go on forever, all by itself.

If you do nothing, it will almost inevitably break down. You do not have to destroy it. It will dissolve by itself because of change.

A friend of mine recently was shaken. His wife wanted a divorce. "I do not know why she wants a divorce," he said. "I didn't do anything!"

That is exactly why she wanted a divorce: he did nothing.

You have to do *something*. You have to maintain your marriage.

What does it mean to "maintain" a marriage?

I got an insight talking to one of my clients.

We were scheduling my visits to his company. I schedule them a year in advance. When I suggested a certain date, he said he could not make that date because he would be on his honeymoon. Honeymoon? I was shocked. When did he divorce his wife? We had just been together for dinner the other evening. Now he was planning to remarry and embark on a honeymoon?

He saw the surprise on my face and, with a smile, calmed me down.

"It is with my present wife. On the anniversary of our marriage every year, we have a fresh, new honeymoon. Because (and here is the important message):

"One honeymoon is not enough for a lifetime of marriage."

Once a year on or near your wedding anniversary, go on a new honeymoon. No children. No one else. Just the two of you. Select the most romantic place you know—an old one that the two of you go back to, or a new one you both want to explore.

Moreover, if you have a rocky marriage, one that is very stressful for whatever reason, take a long weekend away from home, away from stress, from work, from the kids. Go somewhere and be together. Slow down. Do nothing. Just relate to each other and agree that it is forbidden to solve any problems during that long weekend.

Just be with each other. Replenish the batteries.

LAUGHING A LOT

Humor disarms.

I have been observing long-term marriages that seem to be happy marriages and wondering what it is that keeps couples together in this turbulent world we live in, where the divorce rate is high.

I found a common denominator: they laugh a lot. These couples have incredible senses of humor.

Then, I watched some successful executives. The culture in their companies was not as stressed as one would expect. They were really not that sophisticated in their management or leadership, but they had a great sense of humor.

What explains these phenomena?

Humor disarms.

Laughter is evoked when one exaggerates a phenomenon until it looks ridiculous. It becomes like a cartoon. Thus, it is funny.

Humor relaxes. Humor releases negative energy.

If you can laugh at your problems, nothing is so serious that it calls one to suffer.

While in the past I would get into an argument with my spouse over something that might become increasingly heated, I now try to see what is funny in it and react in a way that makes her laugh. When I succeed, she laughs and then hugs me. (Both partners had better have a healthy sense of humor for this technique to work or it can backfire, big time.)

Problems are laughable if you put your mind to it. If you can laugh at yourself, you can overcome much of the travails of modern life . . . I am, of course, not referring to tragedies.

The more serious you are, and thus view the world with a critical attitude, the more you take the world as a burden, the more stress you bring to your life and to your marriage.

Can you take problems not as crises, but just as problems that can be laughed at? If you can make other people laugh, you can disarm them and remove aggression.

Be careful, though. Some laughter is not laughter but is crying in disguise.

PART III

Self-Development

Finding Purpose

What counts is not what we take, but what we leave behind.

If you follow your inner light, your purpose, when you are breathing your last breath and somebody asks you whether you feel any remorse or sorrow that you wasted your life, you should be able to say, "No, I lived my life to the fullest; I lived the life I was destined to live."

WE ARE BORN AND DIE TWICE

You are what you feel.

In this world, we end up dying twice: once physically, and the second time if no one remembers us anymore.

We are also born twice. Once physically, and the other when we realize why we were born.

In his book *Inner Engineering*, Indian guru Sadhguru deals with two questions: "Who am I?" and "What is my purpose in life?"

Here is my take.

The world is a huge system, composed of endless subsystems that interrelate. No parts of the system live in isolation. We humans do not interrelate only among ourselves but also with nature—the trees that give us oxygen to breathe and the oceans that enable fish to breed, multiply, and feed us. These are just a few examples. Everything we see is interrelated with everything else (whether we are able to observe it or not).

So, who am I? I am what I do to others. I am a father if I perform the roles a father should perform in parenting. Or as the Serbian expression says, "a mother is not the one who gave birth but the one that raised the child."

Our interrelationships are interdependent. Every part of the system can benefit from other parts of the system in one way or another. That is called ecology. In this interdependence, we either enrich or damage each other. A child is dependent on his parents to survive, but the parents need the child to satisfy the need to parent, to have continuation of the chain called a family.

We enrich each other when we are constructive. We destroy each other when we are destructive.

Love is constructive. Hate is destructive. (You can, however, destroy the old to build a better new—that would be *tough love*.)

The purpose of life is in the choice we make about how to interrelate with others.

Do we want to do what we do out of love or out of hate? Out of faith or out of fear? Is it to love, to build, to contribute—to leave a world at least a bit better than the one we found when we were born for the second time? Or, as with some who have destruction as a purpose of their life, to ruin it?

To be constructive, I believe, you need to feel. If you really could feel a chicken and you are asked to behead it, you would not do it. On the other hand, thinking with a dead heart can lead you to carry out destructive actions. The mind can justify many actions that the heart will prohibit. You can always justify something with your thoughts. And those thoughts are not just yours. They are an amalgamation of many influences you have accumulated over the years. Ideologies and indoctrination program the mind and dull the heart, and the result is Auschwitz. So, who are you really? It is not what you think. It is what you feel. What you feel is genuinely yours. And in order to feel, you need to stop thinking.

You are what you feel you are doing to others.

RESPONDING TO THE CALL

To be happy, be who you are.

Reiki says that all human beings have a destiny. How do we discover what our destiny is? By listening to the "call," and by not turning away from that call.

How do you know what the call is?

Here is the insight: When you respond to the call, you get energy. When you do something else, you lose energy.

When you respond to the call, you accept your destiny, your purpose in life. You are inspired (in the spirit).

When I was studying for my Ph.D., I had to choose which field I would specialize in. At that time, operations research was in vogue. Management was in decline as a field of study. I was warned that there was not enough rigorous mathematical modeling in management theory. It was too soft. Everyone recommended that I keep away from it. "There are no jobs teaching management," I was told.

But in my heart, I knew that was what I loved. Thinking about why and how things happen in organizations is what keeps me awake at night and gives me pleasure. I followed my call and did what my heart—not my head—told me to do.

And I did the right thing. I have never "worked." I am always in wonder that people are willing to pay me for having the pleasure of helping them solve their problems. When I lecture or write or consult, I have more energy at the end of the day than when I started. It is as if I am rewarded for serving a purpose I was born to serve.

What is your passion? I have a client who is a billionaire, owning yachts in both the Pacific and the Mediterranean, private jets and houses around the world. I once asked him: "How would making another billion dollars change your life?" He replied: "It's not the billion dollars. It is like mountain climbing. You climb a mountain because you love to climb mountains. That's who you are: a mountain climber. It's not being at the top of the mountain, which is always gratifying, it's the act of conquering the mountain that gives me energy."

What's your "mountain"? What fills you up? What makes living worthwhile?

That is what you should do. And do the best you can. Without wanting, without expecting. Just DO the best you can and if it doesn't work, look for the reason and learn how to do better next time. Life is teaching you, like falling off a bicycle. What did you learn? How to ride it better next time.

Remember: people who love what they are doing are more productive, more innovative, and more pleasant to live and to work with. And they love themselves, too.

LIFE IS VALUED BY HOW WE DIE

Leave the world with more love in it.

Master Chariji was eighty-seven years old when I met him in 2014 in Chennai, India. He was also seriously ill, and his days were numbered. So, I wondered, what does a person who knows that his days are numbered, who faces the inevitable, what does he think is really important in life?

I tended to think that a person in that situation would be evaluating his life, having insights regarding what could have been done differently, better. The person would probably refocus on what really counts in life, so that those days that are left to live were not wasted.

Sitting next to Master Chariji, I asked: "Master, what is really important to you now?"

As I say, I expected some deep insight about life, a kernel of knowledge that I assumed a person facing death would have. That he would try to do something in his last days that he failed to do while still young.

His answer: "Nothing new. The same."

This made me reflect on how integrated he was. He had no remorse about anything he did in his life, and there was no need to change anything in the time left. He did his best at the time. So no remorse. He was living in the present. To him, past and future were all in the present. Or, said differently, the past continued through the present and into the future. There was no difference. He was totally at peace with himself. Nothing needed to change. There was no waste in the past that he needed to correct in the present before the future evaporates. What is, is. What was meant to be was meant to be. Free. Free from remorse. Free from guilt. Free from wishful thinking. Free to live. Free to die peacefully.

"Life is valued by how we die," he said.

Next, I asked Master Chariji if I would be able to see him privately.

"If I can be of service to you, yes," he said.

This triggered another profound insight in me: he was dying, and he was ready to give from the scarce minutes left, to serve me or anyone else. This surprised me, as my perception was that old people become selfish, cherishing every second of life left to be used by, and for, themselves, avoiding wasting it on others.

Why was Chariji's answer different? Because it came from the heart and was full of love. And to love is to give of yourself to others at any time, if needed.

Do *tikkun olam*. Heal the world. Look beyond yourself and serve. In this way, you'll find peace, and leave the world with more love in it than you encountered when you were born.

WHEN DOES LIFE END?

To be alive forever . . .

Imagine a person sitting in a room full of people debating a subject. This person does not say a word. Does not express anything, even through body language.

You would say that this person is not *really* there. Physically yes, but that is all.

Now imagine the same room with the same people debating a subject and repetitively quoting someone who already died. Is that "someone" in the room? Not physically, but otherwise they are fully engaged in the discussion and "alive." As I noted earlier, we die twice: once physically and the second time when no one remembers us.

Some people pass through life unnoticed. They have been here physically, but when they perish physically, they perish totally. In Isabel Allende's novel *Eva Luna*, this is expressed in words the narrator's mother once shared with her: "There is no death, daughter. People die only when we forget them."

Is Buddha alive? Not physically, but interactively very much so. Is Jesus Christ or Moses alive? For sure. Even Hitler is alive with the rise of the neo-Nazis around the world. How about Frida Kahlo or Marie Curie? Alive. Karl Marx? I would say he is either dead or dying.

To remain alive, one has to do something while physically alive. Then, upon death, a certain spirit is left behind that continues to impact the world we departed. How long it continues depends on how impactful that something was while the person was physically alive.

What is that "something"?

The more you love and are loved, or hate or are hated, the longer you "live."

Gandhi will be remembered for generations to come. Jesus's love was so enormous that it is forever. Unfortunately, so is Hitler's spirit.

If love or hate continue after our death, apparently, there is "life" after death, too. "Life" is here in quotation marks to indicate that it is a different life, not a life of thinking but a life of feeling. With no body, no mind, and thus no limitations.

Love or hate are perpetual, ageless. There is no body. No mind. No past. And no future either. The body dies, but feelings continue. People still feel you after you are gone. If you are loved, they still love you after your body is gone. If you spread hate, for them you are still alive, too.

Thus, there is no need to be scared of death. We are finally free from the tyranny of thoughts and the pains of the body. Free to only feel. To feel without limitations, without expecting anything in return. Because out there, there is no return.

The question is: How do we want to be remembered? What feelings do we want to leave behind?

If it is love, your spirit is free to go. If it is hate, it lingers around, hoping for forgiveness.

Why?

At the end of the day, we all seek harmony. We live to love and be loved. Rejection is painful, and a person who dies but feels rejection and hate will suffer and try to find a way to be forgiven.[1]

LIVE AS IF YOU WILL DIE TOMORROW

Resolve to do your best.

The expression "live as if you are dead" teaches us something important: when you die, nothing matters anymore and everything you thought was important while being alive becomes useless.

Nothing matters anymore. Nothing perturbs you. When you are dead, you are in eternity and there is no way to come back and fix the problems that you created when you were alive.

Why do we work ourselves to death on issues that in the long run—when we die—do not count, do not matter?

One reason may be the denial of death and of our mortality. The result is humans act as if they will live forever and end up wasting their lives on things that in the long run don't matter.

The next time you have a problem, ask yourself this question: Will it matter when I'm gone forever? Will it matter even five years from now?

[1] In my memoir, *The Accordion Player: My Journey From Fear to Love*, I describe my simulated death experience and how I discovered life after death.

This way of thinking might give you a tool to help you filter out what to worry and care about and what to just shrug your shoulders at—resolving to do your best, and then letting go.

LEARN AS IF YOU WILL LIVE FOREVER

When you stop growing, you start dying.

No one lives forever, but who knows when any of us will part company with this world? You might live a long life, so why not keep learning and improving who you are? The more you know, the more you know how much you do not know. There is endless opportunity to learn.

But, to learn, you need to allocate time.

Why is it important to allocate your time? We know from physics that time is endless. It was born with the Big Bang, and it has been going on ever since. Since it's scary to think about death, we behave as if time were endless, as if we were going to live forever.

If, as an exercise, you estimate how many days you have left on earth, you will feel how extremely valuable what you do with this limited asset—time—becomes.

Open your calendar. What if you budget time just as you budget money? Assume you have 100 percent of your time to allocate. Some of it you need to sleep and eat. Of the time left, what portion of it do you want for integration, for love? Start with loving yourself, with meditation every day, maintaining your health, exercising, and eating healthy, and having appropriate doctor visits. Next, how much love are you going to share with your partner? You need time together. Then, if you're a parent, with the children.

Notice how the sequence goes from the inside out. First comes you; then comes immediate family—partner and children; next, one-on-one relationships; and then extended family and close friends.

Another priority after securing time for integration could be putting things in order.

Having order in your life, having the right things in the right places. Have budgets and knowing where you're spending your money so you aren't caught by surprise. Letting papers on your desk accumulate may leave you totally lost and confused. That will waste your energy. Plan when you are going to sit down and organize your papers and whatever else you need to do—your budgets, your contacts. Let's assume you do that every Monday morning.

What would your third priority be?

To improve yourself: to learn, to grow. Otherwise, you'll be aging mentally. Keep your mind active, keep your spirit active, and you will prolong your life. It doesn't have to be every week or every day. You can say, "Every three months I'm going to take a course, learn something new." Or, "I'm going to read a book every evening." That keeps you growing because when you stop growing, you start dying. Your last priority should be to work to build your assets.

Notice how the sequence I recommend is the opposite of how people commonly allocate time in the modern world. Their first priority is to increase material assets, with excessive time allocated to work. Only if there is time left is it dedicated to getting organized, and subsequently, if there is still any time left, it is allocated to lifelong learning. Self-integration and integration of the family and community, and so on, is the last priority. No wonder families and people are getting wealthier while falling apart.

Giving material needs the highest priority was the right sequence in a world of scarcity and is thus still appropriate for underdeveloped economies. But for the developed world, the behavior should be based not on scarcity but on abundance. Working to accumulate wealth should be the last and not the first priority.

At the end of every month, you should compare what you budgeted to what you actually did with your time. Granted, there's always going to be a deviation from the plan, so ask yourself how to correct it next month. When you're on your deathbed, you don't want to say, "Ah, I built a big empire. I left a lot of money for my children, but I don't know my children."

Manage your life, manage your time, or your problems will manage you.

LOVE NOW

The name of God, in the Jewish religion, is Yehove.

In Hebrew, when you have the letter *yod* (the "y") in front of a verb, it means it will be done in the future. *Hove* means "now."

The name of God is "Make Your Future Today."

Do not live in the past and feel miserable ("I should have . . ." and "why didn't I . . . ?"). Nor live in the future ("I will be happy when . . ."). Be happy now. Love now.

I remember sitting next to my mother's hospital bed just before she died. She was not conscious. Her eyes were open; they were glassy but there was an effort there, or that is what I thought, an effort to see, to hold on.

I tried to imagine what she was feeling during those last moments on earth. Trying to see, trying to have just one more second with someone she loved. What would she have given to see me, to hold onto me? For just one more second.

I found myself wondering, if I were dying, what would I give to hold onto life and see the people I love next to me for just one more second? But then, why wait until I'm dying to live my life surrounded by those I love and who love me?

And love what you do. Everything you do. Stop whatever offends your body organs and whatever offends you spiritually. Emotionally. Socially.

If life is a fixed number of breaths, for every breath you take to hate there is one less to love.

Just Thinking

You can learn from anything and everything.

You don't learn only in school. Life with its challenges is an ongoing school and you are your own teacher. I think the Muslim religion says the day you did not learn is a day you did not live.

When my kids were young, putting them to sleep instead of reading them a book, sometimes I would ask them, "What did you learn today?" When you finish a book, ask yourself that question.

There are no failures in life. you either succeed or you learn.

LIFE IS A GAME OF CARDS

I recently heard the expression "You have to play the cards you're dealt," and it reminded me how true that is—how similar life really is to a game of cards—in multiple ways.

First, you can't control how many cards there are, nor which ones you get. Any attempt to control it (like hiding a card up your sleeve) is cheating. You have to play the cards given to you. Sometimes you get good cards. Sometimes they are lousy.

And, just like in life, evaluating each card alone will not give you an accurate view of what you have. The cards are interdependent.

The value of each card is determined by its importance to the whole hand.

And isn't that like life? Every new situation has its threats and its opportunities. There are strengths and there are weaknesses. See the totality. Do not overlook the forest by focusing on a single tree.

Now, what happens when you get lousy cards? You fold and wait for the next round, right? That is how life should be taken: fold and wait for the next round. There's no use complaining to the dealer. It's not productive to get depressed or angry about the cards you've been dealt. They are what they are. If necessary, fold and look forward to the next round. As another expression goes, "Whenever a door closes, a window opens."

Here is another moral we can learn from playing cards. If you get bad cards in one round and decide to fold, make sure you don't also fold your spirit. If you make the mistake of getting all worked up, you might be given a good set of cards in the next round, yet be so distracted by the last round that you miss an opportunity to win.

Remember: Each round is brand-new.

Come to think of it, how many people have difficulty developing a bond with someone new because they were hurt in a previous relationship? How many people have difficulty starting a new job because the last one was a disaster?

Life presents you with a series of "hands." Just play the ones you're dealt, and remember that each round is a new round, with brand-new opportunities to win—as well as new opportunities to fail.

Enjoy the game. Enjoy life, in spite of its ups and downs—or, perhaps, because of them.

Another lesson: Always make sure to look around and ask yourself, What game are we playing? What is at stake here? What are the rules of this game? What does it mean to win?

Think about the many military people who retire and go to work for a business corporation—neglecting to make a crucial switch in their heads: to realize that now they are playing a different game. Or businessmen who go into politics. It is not the same game. The rules are different, and so are the criteria for "winning."

Furthermore, you must always know who the players are and how many of them are playing. You cannot play solo, in cards or in life, so it is crucial to identify the players and the stakeholders.

How many times have we lost a "round" because we were dealing with person A at the table, only to find out later that the one who was actually calling the shots was someone else—someone who was not even "at the table."

Last analogy: Once you identify the players, learn their style. Find out what drives them. Observe their strategy; often that will tell you what cards they have and what they are looking for. After all, they, too, must play the cards they were dealt.

Some people do not like to play cards. That's okay. You can skip playing card games, but you cannot skip playing the cards of life.

SUCCESS IS TO HAVE SUCCESSFUL FAILURES

Each failure is a success if you learn from it.

Life is never smooth and free of troubles. Life *is* change, and change produces new challenges one needs to address. To address them, one needs to make decisions in situations of uncertainty, and the implementation of such decisions is risky.

Thus, change spells problems.

So?

I, for one, have never heard of a person who overcame all problems without ever making a mistake. To me, even God admits to making a mistake by bringing on the flood; God admits to being powerless to make us all righteous, thus the flood was the wrong decision and God makes a covenant to never repeat that mistake again. God also admits of being forgetful. He brings the rainbow to remind him to stop the rain (Genesis 6:9–9:19). God appears to me so human. So, who is this human who is better than God and never makes a mistake? We consider mistakes failures because we assume we should not have made a mistake.

Since life (change) produces a string of problems and their solutions often do not work out, one can say life is full of failures.

Right?

Not so.

It depends on how you handle failures. If you brood, accuse, and judge yourself for being a failure, then you are right. You are a failure. You failed yourself. You were the victim, the prosecutor, and the judge, all in one.

Real success depends on how successfully you handle your failures.

Getting up means that each problem, each failure, is an invitation to learn something you did not know before.

The more you learn from mistakes, the wiser you become. The wiser you become, the fewer mistakes you will repeat. And how do you really learn? By experience, and that means not being afraid to make mistakes—as long as you learn from them.

Success is not how little you fall. It is how fast you get up.

INTEGRATE THE OPPOSITES

One needs to have both flexibility and control.

One can learn from anything and everything. Not just from books.

Years ago, yoga taught me the need to be flexible and in control at the same time. That gave me an insight into understanding lifecycles that I explore in my book *Managing Corporate Lifecycles*.[1] When an organization is young, it is flexible but does not have much control over what it does. Once the organization ages and reaches the later part of the lifecycle, it has developed control but lost flexibility. To be in your prime, you need to have both flexibility and control.

While practicing yoga, I had another new insight. I learned how one might successfully handle two other incompatible forces: in this case, rigidity and relaxation.

These seem like natural states that go in unison: when you tighten your body you automatically "tighten" your mind, too—you stop thinking; you take a hard breath in and hold it. The opposite is true as well: when you relax your body, you will relax your breathing, too, and vice versa.

In yoga, you learn to integrate opposites, to tighten your body while relaxing with deep breathing.

This gave me insight into how we should lead. "Speak softly and carry a big stick" a West African proverb that Theodore Roosevelt made famous. The more stern you have to be with people, the more relaxed should be your tone of voice and manner of delivering the message. Give a bad-tasting pill in a tasty cocoon. Make a firm request and insist others impeccably implement the decision while using a relaxed tone of voice. It can be casual—even friendly—while at the same time, being firm in the request.

[1] Adizes, I. *Managing Corporate Lifecycles.*

It is a challenge! But, as in yoga, do so by controlling your breathing. Breathe slowly in and slowly out, and do not hold your breath. Once you relax, go and deliver your stern message.

THE SPRING OF YOUTH

Love gives you energy. Hate takes it away from you.

When writing my book on corporate lifecycles,[2] I wondered why systems, people, and organizations have a lot of energy when growing while aging systems have little to no energy.

It was a subject that became very relevant to me as I started to feel my age.

I think I've found an answer.

My formula of success—any way you define success—is helpful in answering the question.

Success = f (external integration / internal DISintegration)

Since energy is fixed at any point in time, the energy has to be allocated to both internal and external integration. Whatever is used by one of them is not available for the other one.

When we are young, we start life by being very integrated physically. When we are born, all subsystems are together at equal age—they are at the starting point—so all organs are "together." All available energy is to be spent on external opportunities. And young kids are full of energy, jumping all over the place. They are very energetic.

Our body organs have fixed but different lifespans. Like all material things, with wear and tear some start functioning less effectively than others.

[2] Adizes, *Managing Corporate Lifecycles.*

Since each organ has a different lifespan, with the passage of time the body starts to disintegrate as a system, and the body needs to dedicate energy to deal with this disintegration, to make the system work in spite of it. The energy that was spent in our youth externally gets redirected as we age to integrate us internally. The result: We are less energetic externally.

How can we retard aging?

The genetic lifespan cannot be changed. It decides just how long you have to live, which is determined by the lifespan of your most critical organs. Maybe, with superb health care, a year or two can be added. Like a car whose engine has a lifespan of XYZ miles, with good care you could possibly add an extra few thousand miles or so, but that would be it.

While you cannot extend your life, you can definitely shorten it with accelerated physical, mental, or social disintegration. When that happens, your externally dedicated energy goes to take care of this disintegration and you age and die prematurely. Have a divorce and see what it does to your lifespan. Or stay married in a seriously dysfunctional marriage.

The way, then, to retard aging is to watch for causes of disintegration. Like stress. That is a big energy consumer. Like wear and tear due to travel and time-zone changes, sleep deprivation, or a diet that is destructive to your organs.

What integrates?

Love.

Do you realize that people who are in love look younger, more radiant? And people that hate look older, washed-up.

The way to retard aging—not to prolong life but to not die younger than the genetic code determines—is to love.

Do you love your job, spouse, car, home, city, country, parents, even your shoes? Everything counts. Everything either gives, or takes away, energy. The more love in your life, the longer you will live and the younger you will feel.

WHEN TO GIVE, WHEN TO TAKE

Never lose your passion to contribute to whatever is bigger than you.

I notice when an organization is young, not necessarily in chronological age, but behaviorally, the people in that organization are prone to give. They're working hard to build an organization to achieve a mission. They're all "giving." Giving energy.

As an aging organization stops building, stops changing, loses its mission, stops growing, the energy of the people that compose it converts itself to taking rather than giving. Everybody is trying to milk the organization, which accelerates its death. The stockholders want maximal dividends, management wants maximum take-home income, and the workers, maximum benefits and salary increases. Everybody acts like hyenas starting to pull out of the organization a piece of meat.

And the same thing apparently applies to human beings. When we are young, behaviorally, we are enthusiastic. We have a mission. We want to change the world. We want to do something different. We give ourselves to the organization, to our relationships, to the world. We work hard on the external environment.

When we start aging, we realize our days are short, not many days left. And we start thinking, What am I going to do with the rest of my life? Giving is not exciting because subconsciously we realize, I think, that we are not going to benefit from that contribution that we are going to be making. And we start looking at how to enjoy life, how to benefit from life, how to experience life before it's too late. And we move to taking, taking from life, traveling, enjoying rather than sacrificing our limited time left for a future we will not enjoy. We might do some small philanthropic work just not to feel guilty, but that's where it ends. Most of it is taking. That's why some older people, no matter how rich they are, are stingy. They don't like to give. They like to keep. This is reflected in their daily life, too. They conserve their energy, which is in decline.

But it doesn't have to be that way.

Age is not only chronological. It's behavioral, too.

I know people in their nineties that are still giving. They're trying to find out what else they can do in the days left with their life to still contribute and make a better world. They're young in spirit.

One way to find out whether you're young or old is looking at how much are you giving versus how much are you taking. And there is a conclusion here: you want to live longer, to live as a young person in spite of being physically older, never lose your passion to contribute to whatever is bigger than you.

Plant a tree, although you know you will not live long enough to be in its shade.

THE TREES OF KNOWLEDGE AND LIFE

Descending from Purgatory to Hell.

According to the Bible, when we were in the Garden of Eden, we were not conscious. Then, after eating from the Tree of Knowledge, we became conscious, and from that point on we needed to understand. We needed to know, and throughout the ages, this need evolved endlessly.

And in my judgment, that is what distinguishes us from other living beings.

No other living creature has formal educational institutions and research labs. We became scientists, forever trying to understand nature, to understand chemistry, biology, zoology, and physics. We also became social scientists—trying to understand history, society, anthropology, and literature. For what we could not explain, we developed philosophy: the philosophy of history, the philosophy of science, the philosophy of any field. And when we had no explanations, we used religion for explanation: "It is God's will" or "the Devil made me do it," and so on. We ate from the Tree of Knowledge. We need to know.

Different people interpret what they know differently from others, and some are adamant about their interpretation—they feel they are right and all others are wrong. We now do not agree on what we know, nor what we should do. There is conflict—some of tragic proportions, as in war and famine. And we are not that happy. We are knowledgeable but unhappy.

Violating God's will and his clear instructions according to tradition, eating from the Tree of Knowledge did not send humanity to Hell, only to purgatory. To descend now to Hell, it is required to eat from the second forbidden tree, the Tree of Life.

We are starting to bite some of the fruit of that second forbidden tree. We are creating life. We are developing technologies to clone animals and, soon, people. We are re-engineering our vegetables and wheat and fruit. And before long we will engineer what we want in a child. Not only the sex, but also the DNA to get a desired appearance and character. And from time immemorial we have also decided to control life by controlling death. By executing people. So, we make and end life. *We*. Humans.

In the first chapter of the Old Testament, when God created humans, God commanded humans to go and rule the animals and the planet. But we did not stop there. Now we are challenging God. We make and end life ourselves. We are replacing God. And the more omnipotent the political ideology, the more it negates God. Fanatics of religions that negate diversity and the seeking of a common goal do not serve God any more than communism does, although they may claim to.

I believe this may end up badly. We may end up in Hell.

Imagine the world with a non-dying population, a non-aging population, surviving mostly on human-implanted devices? Imagine this world. And overall, we are destroying the world we live in: polluting the air, the water, and the earth. We are acting as if we are beyond God.

Our children will have to go to a zoo to see animals that today we can still see all around us. Our grandchildren will never see some of the flowers whose scents we appreciate today because they are becoming extinct this moment. They will never see certain species of fish and birds. Because of air pollution, they will never stand atop a city skyscraper and see an urban panorama stretching for miles in every direction.

So, back to the question: Is it a better world?

I suggest that it is not. Because we've lost sight of the real goal.

What should be our goal?

On Deciding

Don't believe everything you think.

On a bumper sticker, California

As change accelerates in modern life, we are confronted with the need to make decisions faster and faster. It is stressful. Here are some insights on how to handle this challenge.

LISTEN TO THE HEART

Making a decision exclusively with the mind will produce an incomplete decision. If your heart is not in it, you will not feel sure of your decision. By the same token, do not make decisions with just your heart. When you follow only feelings, you might make a decision not based on reason but based only on faith or fear. Neither might give the right answer.

In making a decision, it is necessary to employ both mind and heart.

Notice the feelings about the decision as well as whether it makes logical sense or not.

This shouldn't be done simultaneously. Begin with the heart and check how the decision to be made makes you feel. If it does not feel right, abort. If it is okay, proceed to the head, and analyze cost versus value. When finished, return to the heart. Does what you have just decided still feel okay? If not, abort. If yes, go for it.

Let the heart win. That is the true you.

There is a Montenegrin expression: "*Ko peva zlo ne misli*" ("Whoever sings cannot have malicious thoughts."). When you sing, are you singing with your head or with your heart? Are you thinking or feeling? The heart cannot, ever, be malicious. Only the mind can potentially be. *The heart is always right.*

THE BEST DECISION YOU CAN MAKE

Make a list to reduce uncertainty.

Some people—usually extroverted, creative types—attempt to do too much at once. Their ambition makes them want to do just everything, and they end up overwhelmed by how much there is to do. Fearing making a mistake, they panic.

When people get panicky and they're scared of making a mistake, most of their energy goes to handling the panic. Very little energy is left to deal with the problem they are panicky about.

If you find yourself in that place, the first thing to do is take a deep breath and relax.

The next step is to take a piece of paper and write down ALL the things you need to do. All the things you believe you should do. All the decisions you believe you should make. And don't stop until it is a complete list, including mundane things such as doing laundry. The list should include all the choices, all alternatives. Everything.

Part of the anxiety and panic comes from feeling overwhelmed, perceiving the list to be endless. The moment there is a complete list, uncertainty is reduced and panic might subside.

Next, when you're in a crisis mode like this, don't prioritize your list by how strategic the item is, which usually deals with the long range. When you're under short-term distress, it's useless to think about the long range. What you really need to do is to arrange the list by time sensitivity: What is the most urgent thing I have to do now, and what can wait?

Then look again at every item on your list of urgent things to do, and ask yourself a question: Does it *really* need to be done? Or am I only thinking it *should* be done? Or, I just *want* this to be done? Consider the *need* only: Does this really *need to* be done *now*? The list is now narrower.

Now you must choose what to do from this narrowed-down list of decisions. This is where some people, afraid of making a mistake, freeze up. Ask yourself what is the value you will get from making that decision versus the worst cost if it is a mistake. Judge and decide. Obviously if the cost is higher than the value, skip this choice. And if the value is higher than the cost, put it on your list to do. This does not mean you will do it; it means it is now a candidate to be dealt with.

What if the potential mistake is a very serious one? In that case, seek advice from someone you trust who has no self-interest in which decision you will make. Listen to them, but feel in your stomach if what this person recommends seems right.

Trust your intuition. If it does not feel right, that is good enough reason for you not to do it. You do not need to know why it does not feel right. Put the issue aside. Revisit after a few days and reevaluate. If it still does not FEEL right, skip it. If it now feels acceptable, put it on the list of candidates for action.

The body is a storage bank of information. Sometimes the body reacts to a decision because of past experiences or judgments. The intuition needs to be articulated to be understood, but at this stage it is just a hunch. Do not dismiss intuition. It is valid.

If you cannot get a decision you feel comfortable with, keep looking for other points of view from people you trust until you hit on a direction you feel committed to pursuing. Meditation is a good vehicle to arrive at such a decision. During meditation, issues clear up by themselves. Your heart will tell you what is right.

You should have now a list of candidates for action. Check: do you have the time to do them all? If so, move on. If not, prioritize by how important they are to you, or maybe there is a sequence in which they should be dealt with; often one decision impacts another one on the list, so follow the logic. Another criteria for prioritizing could be just what you like to do versus what you hate to do. Use whichever criteria makes sense to you to prioritize the various decisions you have to make and/or implement.

Let's now assume you made the decision. What should be done next?

Monitor the implementation—maybe it was indeed a mistake—so you can take corrective action in time.

What happens in a company is not what is expected, but what is inspected.

In any case, even if it is too late to prevent more damage, ask yourself: Did you learn a lesson from this situation so the mistake won't be repeated in the future?

The decision itself, with the bad outcome, was NOT the mistake. You made your best effort to make the best decision you could have made at the time. Only later did you realize it was not the right decision. But you cannot reverse the calendar and go back in time to reverse the decision. At the time, you did the best you could have done. Thus, at that time, it was not a mistake. If it was a mistake and you knew it, you would not have chosen that decision.

We really do not make mistakes if we do our absolute best.

The mistake is not in the decision made. It is in not learning from the bad decision.

RESPECT AND SUSPECT

We don't learn from people who agree with us.

An old Hebrew maxim by the Jewish sages says, "*kabdehu ve hashdehu.*" Translated, it means: "Respect and suspect." Let's try to understand this prescription.

Immanuel Kant said that to respect is to recognize the sovereignty of the other person to think differently; to respect is to give the other person space to be who they are, to let them speak their mind freely.

Now, why should we give other people space to think differently? Because we can learn from their difference of opinion. We don't learn from people who agree with us. They only reinforce what we think, and what we think can be a big error. If two people agree on everything, they have nothing to learn from each other.

I appreciate it when people disagree with me and win the argument. It means I learned something I didn't know before the interaction. I consider learning a blessing and, in the case of pointing out to me the mistake I was going to make, I am thankful that I learned before I unintentionally made a bad decision.

In Hebrew, the word "respect" (*kavod*) can be substituted with the word "value" (*haaraha*). Respect has to come before the value created from an interaction can be noted. Showing disrespect discourages the other party from opening up and having the willingness to allocate energy to argue. The opportunity to learn from disagreements is then missed. That's why it is not possible to learn from people we disrespect, or who show disrespect to us. It blocks our thinking and it's difficult to relate to them.

Why do the sages suggest to "suspect"?

Because interests play a significant role in decision making, too. We all have different interests. What you want may not be what I want. Your self-interest might not be my self-interest. We might have a conflict of interests, and your disagreement might be to advance your interests at my expense.

When you interact with people, you must respect them. Try to see whether you can learn from their differences of opinion. But at the same time, in the back of your mind, suspect: Those differences of opinion, are they driven by differences in knowledge and judgments, or by self-interest? If you suspect someone's contribution to the discussion is self-serving, you don't have to buy what they say.

We learn, and thus make better decisions, when a diversity of styles contributes differing opinions, judgments, and information—but only when it is based on common interest.

So, in a debate, the first step is to ask yourself, what is driving the person debating you? Is it self-interest, or is it differences in knowledge and judgment? Respect but, at the same time, suspect, too.

THE DANGERS OF ASSUMING

> *A person is driving his car down a windy road, late at night when it's pitch dark. Then he realizes he has a punctured tire. When he pulls over to try to change the tire, he discovers that he doesn't have a jack. He's*

stuck. He's waiting for cars to pass by so he can ask for a jack, but it's so late at night that there are no cars.

He looks down the road and sees, some distance away, the light of a house. He decides to walk to the house and ask if they can lend him a jack. As he's walking, he starts to envision the conversation: I go and knock on the door. Somebody opens the door. I explain my situation and ask for a jack.

In his imagination, the homeowner asks, "Why are you here in the middle of the night? Why should I give you a jack?"

The first man pictures himself saying, "Please, I need a jack to fix up my car."

Now he presumes that the homeowner asks, "Why should I trust you? Why do you go on a trip without a jack?"

"Well, look at me," the first man is getting ready to respond. "I'm a reasonable and trustworthy person."

"How do I know?"

All this time that the first man is walking down the road and talking to himself, he's getting angrier and angrier at the person he wants to borrow the jack from. When he arrives at the house, he knocks and, just as the homeowner opens the door, he starts screaming at him: "I don't need your jack! If you don't want to give it to me, never mind!"

The homeowner looks at him in total shock. He doesn't know what's going on.

How frequently do we have a conversation in our heads about an event that has not happened yet? By the time we finish our imaginary debate and analysis with ourselves, in the process of amplifying the case and creating a scenario that fits our way of perceiving reality, we've confused what is going on in our heads with the reality we need to deal with. We're getting all upset while, in truth, nothing has happened yet.

You can see this with some people as they walk into a meeting. They come in bitter, ready for a fight, although nothing has happened yet. They have probably made assumptions about what is going to happen in the meeting, expecting to have some difficult exchanges with people. Now, hurt, they are gearing up for a fight although in reality nothing has occurred—at least, not yet.

Here is a joke about how assumptions can destroy relationships. It's called the "watch syndrome."

> *An old man and a young man are riding a train. After a while, the young man asks the old man, "Sir, what time is it, please?" The old man doesn't answer him. After some more time, the young man asks again, "Sir, please, what time is it?" Again, no answer.*
>
> *Finally, the young man gets upset and says, "Sir, why don't you tell me what time it is? I can see you have a watch. I know you can hear because I overheard your conversation with the conductor. What did I do wrong that you refuse to tell me what time it is?"*
>
> *And the old man says, "Look, young man, I'm going to tell you what time it is, and I'm going to see you're an intelligent young man, and we're going to start a conversation, and it's going to be very interesting, and then we'll get off at the same railway station, and because I had an engaging exchange of ideas with you, I'm going to invite you home for dinner. I have a beautiful young daughter who's going to fall in love with you, and I don't want my daughter to marry a man who doesn't have a watch!"*

We often confuse reality with our imagined reality. We react to fictitious sets of circumstances as if they were real.

I call that the terror of assumptions. In our heads, we assume certain interactions, certain events, which haven't taken place yet. But to us, they are as vivid as if they've already happened, so we react—although they may never come to pass.

I saw once a bumper sticker that said: *"Don't believe everything you think."* It's important to control what we think and evaluate, because we might be making incorrect assumptions that can cause us to behave in a way that can damage our goals.

> *Be curious first, and then judge.*
> *Investigate before you decide.*
> *Do not assume.*
> *Meet others with an open mind, without prejudgment.*

CONFUSING OPINION WITH DECISION

You might ask for an opinion, advice from a person you are close to, and they give you a recommendation. If you then follow your own judgment, ignoring their recommendation, they get upset because you didn't follow their judgment.

They're confusing decision with opinion.

I encounter this problem frequently in the business environment, where a new culture of participative management is being promoted. Leaders are expected to be politically correct.

Some people participate and add opinions but they expect their opinions to be followed. This could disarm and paralyze management, which is ultimately accountable for implementing the decision. Management finds itself in a position in which it feels pressured to follow the consensus, although that might be against its own judgment. It feels pressured to be politically correct, to implement a decision it doesn't believe in.

But this is not just happening in business or with friends. It can get acute and dangerous in a marriage. In today's environment, where equal authority is expected, this misunderstanding can be a serious source of frustration and anger.

When I ask people for their feedback about a decision I'm going to make, I tell them: "I'm asking for your opinion, not for your decision." And when I am asked for an opinion, I make my recommendation. To prevent a dangerous miscommunication—so it is not interpreted as a decision I expect to be implemented, which will carry repercussions if it is not followed—I add the following sentence: "Respectfully, *for your consideration*."

LET GO OF ATTACHMENTS

Whatever you control, or try to control, controls you.

In Heartfulness meditation, a practice taught by the Heartfulness mission in India, and in any meditation practices that I can think of, they all prescribe not being attached. When we meditate, thoughts come up. They should be treated like passing clouds, the prescription being: Don't get attached to your thoughts. Let them pass like clouds in the sky.

How can this principle be put to practice in everyday decision making?

I think I've found an answer in a parable from Buddhism:

> *A farmer walks to the market holding a rope, at the end of which there is a cow. He is asked by the passers-by, "Why are you tied up to the cow? Why is it controlling you?"*
>
> *And he answers, "The cow isn't controlling me, I'm controlling the cow."*
>
> *"Well, if the cow is not controlling you," they respond, "why don't you let go of the rope?"*
>
> *He can't. The cow will wander off.*

Whatever you control, controls you. You are holding each other equally captive.

Notice how assets can imprison a person who has money and assets. They work hard to not lose it. Now who owns whom? As the Hebrew expression says, "*Marbe mamon marbe deaga*," "The more money you have, the more worries you have." It is not just the person controlling the money. It is money now controlling the person and dictating what to do or not to do.

Whatever we try to control, controls us.

Take the case of a famous artist. In the beginning of her career, she wanted to be famous and well respected. Her wishes were granted. She feels she "owns" the audience now. But guess what? The audience owns her, too. She cannot cross a hotel lobby without being mobbed and asked to sign autographs or be photographed with people. She has lost her privacy and control of her time. She owns the public, but the public owns her, too. That's called being attached. The highest level of attachment is "addiction." A person cannot let go of the thing they are trying to control, and what they are trying to control is holding them captive.

Culturally, we are used to the popularized romantic notion of loving someone to the extent of not being able to live without them. This is often at the root of great personal pain, as this love is based on dependency and attachment.

What does dependence really mean?

Lack. Neediness. Shortage. Scarcity. It means you don't have something, and that's why you depend. In the context of love, it means depending on the other person to feel you are loved. It may be because you don't love yourself. You are love-deficient, so you need to "import" it. If you did love yourself, if your beloved leaves for whatever reason, it would be painful for a day or two or a bit longer. But since you love yourself, it would not be as devastating as it would be if you felt destitute, unloved, and in despair because your beloved left and took love with them . . . You still have love. You love yourself.

When you are attached—dependent on getting love from others—you are a prisoner who is fearful of losing that which you are attached to. You are a person who is always on the watch to monitor if the one you love is going to leave. Ironically, these are the fears that typically trigger controlling behaviors—putting pressure on the other person to give and reinforce love continuously. It may end up making the relationship dysfunctional and destroying it. The beloved feels used.

People who lose a love without depending don't lose their lives, because they can still love themselves. They feel the temporary sorrow of losing a loved one, but they are not depleted, defeated, or destroyed—as are those who get love only from external sources.

Not to be attached means to be above any idea, to be free of owning it.

Like in meditation, it means allowing a thought to pass by without elaborating on it, without being interested in it to the point that you own that thought and, in the process of owning it, the thought ends up owning you, and you become its prisoner.

That's why it's so important to be above your point of view. To have no prejudice and remain open-minded. That is what makes you free. Being attached is being a prisoner of what you are attached to. And when you are above any argument, any idea—in other words, looking at it, observing it, noticing it, without feeling that you own it and thus need to offend or defend—you are free to learn, to grow and develop.

My Mantra

Speak without offending.

Listen without defending.

Love without depending.

Live without pretending.

Years ago I was going through some pain. As a Holocaust survivor I had difficulties with the concept of love. And that is how this book came about. And then I came across the above passage on the Internet—its author is unknown (some associate it with Buddhism)—and it gave me a compass to direct me to the right approach to take in life. It became my mantra. I repeat it as I swim my laps. I recite it when I start my meditation.

SPEAK WITHOUT OFFENDING

If you're offending someone, it is because you could be scared of losing an argument. So you launch a preemptive attack. Or you might be scared of not being heard, not being appreciated. You fear that your feelings or ideas are not being given the weight they deserve. Fear could be generated by past experiences that have nothing to do with the present situation, but "past music" in your head does interfere with the music you hear now.

"Speak without offending" can be analyzed through the principle of nonattachment as well. In trying to defend something dear to our hearts—either an argument or a point of view—we may offend the other party. We are attached to the argument, become combative about it, and attempt to win the other person over to our belief. We cannot let go of it. It controls us, and we "oversell" our idea, our prejudice, trying to dominate the other party into accepting our perception. And by doing so we offend, we attack. To speak without offending you need to have no fear. Offending means being angry. And anger comes from fear. So stop stop fearing and you might stop offending.

Ask yourself what is it you fear? And what is so terrible if you lose the argument?

LISTEN WITHOUT DEFENDING

Why are you defending? The same fear applies—that you might lose the argument, and if you lose an argument, it proves you're not as smart as you would like to project yourself to be. Or, again, you feel you're not being listened to or are being dismissed. Defensiveness arises out of the attachment to some idea, and the attempt to convince others of its rightness.

It helps to relax; take a deep breath before you start defending an argument. I would go into meditation before a meeting where I have to defend something that I am emotionally attached to. When you need to defend an argument, if you feel anxiety, it's better not to speak. Just take a deep breath and slowly, slowly approach your argument *de nuevo*, again. With a new approach. Do not repeat your defense. That is how you will get into a shouting match. Explain it differently, slowly. Take a break between points in your argument and see if the other party follows you.

Communicate with a teaspoon, not a fire hose.

LOVE WITHOUT DEPENDING

Once you depend on the love other people give you, you start living in fear that they might leave you, and that's painful. You fight to hold onto the love you so depend on. And as you hold tight, you might be suffocating the other party. You might be limiting their ability to love you of their own volition. Your expectations and demands have turned them into suppliers of love—whether they want to be or not. They might resent it, and from there we slide into the fears and anger that destroy a relationship. What is driving your dependence is expectations. You expect something from your loved one. And you depend on them to provide what you expect.

The best way not to depend is not to expect. It is okay to want but not to expect. Better even not to want either, but that is reserved for the saints.

LIVE WITHOUT PRETENDING

Why are you pretending? Fear that you're not good enough. You are more than good enough if you love yourself. You will accept your deficiencies. When you do not love yourself, when you reject yourself, no matter how good you are, you are never going to feel good.

Some humans live with an ideal self-image they are attached to throughout their life. They cannot let go of that image, which is a fruit of their aspirations, and they live pretending they are actually that person while, in reality, they are not. Or the reverse is true, and they live with a negative self-image. They end up prisoners of a personality of their imagination born from unfulfilled aspirations. Since it is a fake image, when the truth is revealed, a rude, painful awakening usually follows. Your heart knows when you are pretending. Your heart knows when you lie. So in order to be genuine, can you listen and follow your heart?

What is your mantra?

Thank you for being with me on this journey.

The end is the beginning . . .

Ichak K. Adizes
Santa Barbara, California

About the Author

For more than fifty years, Dr. Ichak Kalderon Adizes has developed, tested, and documented the proprietary methodology that bears his name. The Adizes Symbergetic Methodology is used to manage and lead change for exceptional results, effectively and efficiently, and without destructive conflict. *Leadership Excellence Magazine* named Dr. Adizes one of the "Top Thirty Thought Leaders on Leadership," and PRovoke Media (formerly The Holmes Report) named him one of the "Best Communicators Among World Leaders" in 2017—alongside Pope Francis, Angela Merkel, and the Dalai Lama.

In 2019, in recognition of his contributions to management theory and practice, Dr. Adizes received a Lifetime Achievement Award from the International Academy of Management. He has also been awarded twenty-one honorary doctorates from universities in eleven countries.

Dr. Adizes is a former tenured faculty member at UCLA. He has taught as a visiting professor at Stanford University, Tel Aviv University, and Hebrew University, and as a lecturer with the Columbia University Executive Program. He has served as dean of the Adizes Graduate School for the Study of Organizational Therapy and Collaborative Leadership and was an academic advisor to the

International School of Management for the Academy of National Economy of the Russian Federation.

He is the founder of the Adizes Institute, an international change-management company based in Santa Barbara, California, that delivers the Adizes Program for Symbergetic change management to clients in the public and private sectors. In addition to advising prime ministers and cabinet-level officers across the world, Dr. Adizes has delivered the Adizes program to a wide variety of companies ranging from start-ups to members of the Fortune 100.

Dr. Adizes lectures in four languages and has appeared before well over two hundred and fifty thousand senior-level executives in more than fifty-two countries, and several million over the Internet. His book *Managing Corporate Lifecycles* was named one of the "Ten Best Business Books" by *Library Journal*. He is an international bestseller and has published twenty-eight books, translated into a combined total of thirty-six languages.

Dr. Adizes is married with six grown children. Living in Santa Barbara, California, he loves to play the accordion, and practices yoga and Heartfulness meditation.

Visit his website at ichakadizes.com, email him at books@adizes.com, and watch videos on his YouTube channels at youtube.com/c/adizesofficial/ and youtube.com/c/DrIchakAdizes-channel/.

BOOKS BY THE AUTHOR

Publications.Adizes.com

1. Adizes, I. *The Power of Collaborative Leadership*. Forthcoming, 2023.
2. Adizes, I. *Systemic Coaching*. Forthcoming, 2023.
3. Adizes, I. *The Accordion Player: My Journey from Fear to Love*. Newtown, PA: WS Press, 2023.
4. Adizes, I. *What Matters in Life*. Newtown, PA: WS Press, 2023.
5. Adizes, I. *Insights on Socio-Political Issues: Volume III*. Santa Barbara, CA: Adizes Institute Publications, 2019.
6. Adizes, I. *Insights on Personal Growth: Volume III*. Santa Barbara, CA: Adizes Institute Publications, 2019.
7 Adizes, I. *Insights on Management: Volume III*. Santa Barbara, CA: Adizes Institute Publications, 2018.
8. Adizes, I., with Yechezkel and Ruth Madanes. *The Power of Opposites*. Santa Barbara, CA: Adizes Institute Publications, 2015.
9. Adizes, I. *Mastering Change*. Santa Barbara, CA: Adizes Institute Publications, 1992. Revised edition, Adizes Institute Publications, 2015.
10. Adizes, I. *Insights on Management: Volume II*. Santa Barbara, CA: Adizes Institute Publications, 2014.
11. Adizes, I. *Insights on Personal Growth: Volume II*. Santa Barbara, CA: Adizes Institute Publications, 2014.
12. Adizes, I. *Insights on Policy Issues: Volume II*. Santa Barbara, CA: Adizes Institute Publications, 2014.
13. Adizes, I. *Food for Thought: On What Counts in Life*. Santa Barbara, CA: Adizes Institute Publications, 2012.

14. Adizes, I. *Food for Thought: On Change and Leadership*. Santa Barbara, CA: Adizes Institute Publications, 2012.

15. Adizes, I. *Food for Thought: On Management*. Santa Barbara, CA: Adizes Institute Publications, 2012.

16. Adizes, I. *Insights on Management: Volume I*. Santa Barbara, CA: Adizes Institute Publications, 2011.

17. Adizes, I. *Insights on Personal Growth: Volume I*. Santa Barbara, CA: Adizes Institute Publications, 2011.

18. Adizes, I. *Insights on Policy: Volume I*. Santa Barbara, CA: Adizes Institute Publications, 2011.

19. Adizes, I. *How to Manage in Times of Crisis (And How to Avoid a Crisis in the First Place)*. Santa Barbara, CA: Adizes Institute Publications, 2009.

20. Adizes, I. *Leading the Leaders: How to Enrich Your Style of Management and Handle People Whose Style Is Different from Yours*. Santa Barbara, CA: Adizes Institute Publications, 2004.

21. Adizes, I. *Management/Mismanagement Styles: How to Identify a Style and What to Do About It*. Santa Barbara, CA: Adizes Institute Publications, 2004.

22. Adizes I. *Corporate Lifecycles: How Organizations Grow, Age, and Die*. Initial publication by Prentice Hall, 1990. Reprint, Santa Barbara, CA: Adizes Institute Publications. New revised edition: *Managing Corporate Lifecycles: Complete Volume* or *Volume 1 and Volume 2*, Santa Barbara, CA: Adizes Institute Publications, 2004.

23. Adizes, I. *The Ideal Executive: Why You Cannot Be One and What to Do About It*. Santa Barbara, CA: Adizes Institute Publications, 2004.

24. Adizes, I. *Conversations with CEOs*. Santa Barbara, CA: Adizes Institute Publications, 2004.

25. Adizes, I. *The Pursuit of Prime.* Santa Monica, CA: Knowledge Exchange, 1996. Reprint, Santa Barbara, CA: Adizes Institute Publications.

26. Adizes, I. *How to Solve the Mismanagement Crisis.* Homewood, IL: Dow Jones/ Irwin, 1985. Reprint, Santa Barbara, CA: Adizes Institute Publications.

27. Adizes, I., and E. Mann Borgese, eds., *Self-Management: New Dimensions to Democracy.* Santa Barbara, CA: ABC-CLIO, 1975. Reprint, Santa Barbara, CA: Adizes Institute Publications.

28. Adizes, I. *Industrial Democracy: Yugoslav Style.* New York Free Press, 1971. Reprint, Santa Barbara, CA: Adizes Institute Publications.

THE ADIZES INSTITUTE WORLDWIDE

Since its founding in 1970, the Adizes Institute has guided companies to achieve exceptional results by managing change rapidly and without disruptive conflict.

The Institute uses the Symbergetic™ proprietary methodology, developed by Prof. Ichak Adizes. This approach is timeless, unique, and adaptable to every company, no matter the industry, size, or maturity. It represents a paradigm shift from traditional consulting or coaching.

Our programs enable companies to achieve four *simultaneous* goals: solving chronic problems, building teams, leadership training and development, and producing exceptional results. Our clients have included Applied Materials, SanDisk, Bank of America, Royal Dutch Shell, Sberbank, and various governments around the world (see testimonials at Adizes.com).

From offices in various countries, a variety of Change Management services are delivered by Certified Adizes Associates—professionals who are exclusively qualified to deliver the Symbergetic methodology. These services foster and nurture a culture of mutual trust and respect and empower organizations to diagnose their own problems and agree on effective solutions. Those solutions, as our mission states, can be rapidly implemented without destructive conflict.

The Adizes Institute Training and Certification Academy provides training and certification in the methodology to qualified applicants who, by and large, already possess advanced degrees in business or other disciplines and have multiple years of executive experience.

We have documented the theoretical framework of the methodology in twenty-eight books, some translated into as many as thirty-six languages (see Publications.Adizes.com).

We are passionate about and committed to enabling organizations to reach their full potential. We are governed by a code of ethics that pledges us to deliver the best to our clients. Profits are our constraint, not our goal.

For inquiries on the Institute's services, please visit www.adizes.com.